SPREE KILLERS

Al Cimino

Quercus

CONTENTS

INTRODUCTION

On 2 June 2010, taxi-driver Derrick Bird drove around the back roads of West Cumbria in northwest England shooting people. In two hours he had killed 12 and wounded another 11, before killing himself. He was the latest in a long line of spree killers – men, and it is almost always men, who one day just lose it and begin killing those around them.

These are not serial killers, who murder stealthily over a long period while avoiding capture – *they* usually have a sexual motive. Nor are they mass murderers like the SS or the Taliban who have political or religious justifications, however spurious, for what they are doing. With spree killers it is usually impossible to make out any motivation. Few survive to explain their actions. The notes they leave behind are seldom illuminating. The handful that dodge the police bullets and balk at suicide rarely make sense.

Derrick Bird's rampage is typically puzzling. He knew some of his victims, but not others. The first person he killed was his twin brother David, but a few days earlier they had had dinner together and seemed on the best of terms. Next came the family solicitor Kevin Commons. There was talk of a quarrel over a will. The family denied it. Then the killer drove to the taxi rank in Whitehaven where he shot and killed one colleague and injured another. But there is no indication that he had any falling out with his fellow drivers.

After that he seems to have picked victims in the surrounding villages at random. Some he may have known casually, others not at all. There was speculation that Bird had been planning his spree for five years, though family and friends say he was pleasant and mild mannered. Then there was the violent movie, *On Deadly Ground*, which he watched the night before the murders. Could that have stirred up some violent instinct? No one really knows. True, many of these factors come up in other cases, but not consistently so it is difficult to judge their significance.

All we do know is that in the UK, spree killings are rarer than they are in the US. That is because it is harder to obtain firearms in the UK. However, in this book there are killers from all over the world – Canada, Korea, China, Japan, Australia, France, Finland, Germany, New Zealand, Nepal. After Charles Whitman, the sniper in the tower in Austin, Texas, in 1966, it was thought that the phenomenon of spree killing was related to America's involvement in the Vietnam War. But cases of seemingly harmless people suddenly going on a murderous rampage long predate that incident. In 1913, in Germany, Ernst Wagner killed 14 and injured 11, and would have gone on to kill many more if he had not been restrained.

Some spree killers plan their murders in detail long in advance. Others seemingly do it on the spur of the moment. In some cases, people said, after the event, that they knew the perpetrator was about to explode. In others, there were no telltale signs, even with the benefit of hindsight. This book carries 45 profiles of the world's most notorious spree killers, so the reader can see how these shocking events unfold. Perhaps you will be able to detect a pattern and fathom the reasons and motivations behind these terrible atrocities.

ERNST WAGNER

Germany, 4 September 1913

Failed playwright turned mass murderer

At about 11 p.m. on 4 September 1913 40-year-old schoolteacher Ernst Wagner from Degerloch, a suburb of Stuttgart, returned to the village of Mühlhausen in southwest Germany where he had taught 11 years before. He was carrying two Mauser C96 service pistols and 272 rounds of ammunition. Before he began his night's work, he intended to cut the telephone wires to the village, but the poles were high and it was raining heavily. Instead, he set fire to four barns. Then, with his face covered by his wife's veil, he walked through the village, shooting anyone he came across.

Wagner killed eight people immediately. A ninth, Jacob Knötzele, was mortally wounded and died a few hours later. Wagner planned only to kill men, he later said, claiming that the one young girl he killed during the shooting spree was hit by accident.

After firing some 70 bullets and hitting 20 people, Wagner took refuge in a barn, where he shot an ox. Before he could reload from the ammunition pouch on his belt, which still contained 198 cartridges, the villagers overpowered him with pitchforks, sabres and scythes. It was only then that they discovered the crazed assailant had once been their mild-mannered schoolteacher.

One man swung an axe, cutting off Wagner's right hand, and he was left for dead. Around 2 a.m. a policeman arrived to find that he was still breathing. When he came round, Wagner admitted that he had killed his wife and four children earlier that day. He had planned to commit suicide, he said, after he had killed the entire male population of Mühlhausen. As that was now impossible, he expressed the hope that he would be sentenced to death and decapitated. Instead he was found to be insane and confined to an asylum for the rest of his life.

A classic case of paranoia

Wagner was studied by Professor Robert Gaupp of the University of Tübingen, who diagnosed a classic case of paranoia. Born to a promiscuous mother and a drunken father who died when he was two, Wagner had long nurtured the ambition

'To my people: I want the Devil, for I want to make martyrs of everything and everybody within range of my pistol'

to become a playwright. After training to be a teacher, he was sent to the village of Mühlhausen in 1901, when he was 27. It seems that that summer, probably while drunk, he committed an act of sodomy with an animal. He believed that some of the villagers knew about this and he bought a gun so he could resist if he was arrested for bestiality. From then on he was always armed.

Around this time his mother died and Wagner started an affair with the daughter of the owner of the inn where he was staying. She fell pregnant. He was pressured into marrying her, even though he did not love her any more. Considering her a social inferior, he treated her more like a servant than a wife.

In 1902 Wagner was sent to the poor and isolated village of Radelstatten. He considered this a punishment for some unnamed crime. His wife gave him three more children and his growing family proved a burden on his small salary as a schoolteacher. Although he continued to write, his ambition to be a famous playwright now seemed beyond his reach. In despair he attempted suicide, but found himself, he said, too weak to go through with it. Instead he bought the two Mausers and began planning his revenge on those he believed to have been the cause of his failure – the men of Mühlhausen. He spent long hours in the forest at target practice. Ironically, there was no indication that he was bloodthirsty – even the sight of blood made him physically sick.

Stabbed as they slept

For ten years Wagner made repeated requests for a transfer. Finally, in May 1912, he was sent to Degerloch, Stuttgart. But as soon as he got there, he saw hints that people somehow knew of his crime. It was then that he decided to put his plan of revenge into action. Before Wagner began his killing spree in Mühlhausen, he wrote to a Stuttgart newspaper, saying: 'To my people: I want the Devil, for I want to make martyrs of everything and everybody within range of my pistol; but I know that is not always possible. After I have accomplished my purpose, I want to be a martyr, too. For years I have always gone to bed with a dagger.' At 5 a.m. on 4 September 1913 he knocked his sleeping wife unconscious and stabbed her to death. Then he killed their children, stabbing them in the throat and chest as they slept. He did this, he told Professor Gaupp, out of pity. He did not want them to be ridiculed throughout their lives as he had been.

> **VICTIMS**
>
> Anna Friedericke Wagner, *née* Schlecht, age unknown, Wagner's wife
> Klara Wagner, 10, his daughter
> Elsa Wagner, 8, his daughter
> Robert Wagner, 6, his son
> Richard Wagner, 5, his son
> Marie Magdalena Bader, 10
> Georg Friedrich Bauer, 64
> Johann Friedrich Geissinger, 60
> Adolf Heinrich Knötzele, 52
> Johann Jakob Knötzele, 50
> Johann Georg Müller, 54
> Jakob Franz Schmierer, 32
> Christian Thomas Vogel, 65
> Christian Widmaier, 68

Wagner then made his way to his brother's home in Eglosheim outside Ludwigsburg, where he himself had been born. His brother was not there, but Wagner told his wife that he would return later. After the massacre at Mühlhausen, he intended to return and murder his brother, then burn down the house he had been born in before killing himself. He wrote to several people, including his sister, who received a letter that said simply: 'Take poison! Ernst!'

LITERARY OUTPUT

Since his student days, literature had been Wagner's greatest love. He read widely and craved literary success. At first, he wrote poetry, imitating Heinrich Heine whom he later denounced in a fit of anti-Semitism. He then turned to drama, writing plays about the sufferings of Christ and the burning of Rome under Nero. In other plays he cast himself in the role of murderer and arsonist.

When Wagner could find no producer or publisher for his plays, he had them printed at his own expense, though some the printer refused to print, considering them too blasphemous. After a few glasses of beer, Wagner would boast that he was a great dramatist, comparing himself to Shakespeare, Goethe and Schiller. The next day he would return to school teaching in his usual quiet way.

Wagner continued writing while in the asylum. During the First World War he rewrote some of his earlier work as patriotic rants. Seemingly embracing his condition, he wrote a play called *Wahn* – or 'Delusion' – about the life of 'Mad King Ludwig' of Bavaria, which he considered his best work. Again he found no producer for it and resented the fact that his literary output was only of interest to psychiatrists. He began to believe that other writers had stolen his work. The 1907 film *Ben Hur*, he said, was based on his *Pictures from Ancient Rome*. He also maintained that the publication date of others' work had been falsified to hide the fact that they had plagiarized his output. It was all one great Jewish conspiracy to deny him recognition for his genius.

In the asylum Wagner fought to have himself declared sane, so that he could be convicted of murder and executed, even abusing Professor Gaupp for certifying him insane. By the time he reconciled himself to the fact that no retrial would be permitted, the First World War was at its height. Wagner begged to be sent to the front so that he could die for his country. This, too, was denied. He began writing long letters to the German High Command giving them advice. Germany's eventual defeat left him depressed. However, he took a considerable interest in political developments in Germany after the war. In 1929 he joined the Nazi Party, taking great pride in the fact that he was the first inmate of the asylum to do so. He died of tuberculosis in 1938 at the age of 64.

No remorse

Wagner never expressed any regrets about killing either his family or the victims in Mühlhausen. However, he was embittered by the fact that he had been declared insane and been denied fame as a literary figure. The one regret he expressed was that, as a youth, he had admired the work of Romantic poet Heinrich Heine. After embracing the Nazi philosophy, Wagner now repudiated him. Heine was Jewish. Wagner blamed his incarceration on the Jewish lawyer who had defended him at his trial and who was later disbarred when Hitler came to power. Wagner also believed that his lawyer had handed documents about his case to Franz Werfel, a playwright and, later, a Hollywood screenwriter, which Werfel used in a drama about mental illness, produced in Stuttgart. Werfel was, of course, Jewish.

MUTSUO TOI

Japan, 21 May 1938

The Tsuyama massacre

The Tsuyama massacre took place, not in Tsuyama city, but in the rural village of Kaio close by. On 21 May 1938, using a shotgun, a Japanese sword and an axe, 21-year-old Mutsuo Toi killed 30 people, including his own grandmother, and seriously injured three others before killing himself. Until the spree killings by Woo Bum-kon in South Korea in 1982, the Tsuyama attack was regarded as the world's worst massacre by an individual.

Mutsuo Toi was born on 5 March 1917 in Okayama Prefecture in the south of Japan's main island, Honshu. His parents were well off, but they died of tuberculosis while he was still a baby. Mutsuo and his sister went to live with their grandmother in Kaio and were brought up by her. As a child Mutsuo was outgoing, but at 17, when his sister left home to marry, he became withdrawn. This is a social phenomenon, familiar in Japan even today, known as *hikokomori*, meaning to pull away or be confined. It can also be a response to the stress and pressures of life. As far as the neighbours of Mutsuo Toi were concerned, this withdrawal was a particularly dangerous and ultimately deadly development.

In 1936 Mutsuo Toi – and the rest of Japan – became rapt by the story of Sada Abe, a prostitute who had strangled her lover then cut off his penis and carried it around with her. She intended to perform necrophilic acts with it before committing suicide. Her pursuit and arrest became a national sensation. Crowds formed to attend the court case. Her story inspired a slew of books and films. At that time, Mutsuo Toi began writing a novel called *Yutokaiomaru*, or 'Ambitious Enterprise in the Kaio Circle'. The manuscript still exists.

An unwelcome visitor

He took also part in the traditional rural Japanese activity of *yobai* or 'night-crawling'. Young men would creep into the bedrooms of young women at night, slip under the bedclothes and make their intentions clear. If the woman consented, they would make love until the early morning, when he would slip out of the house discreetly. However, it seems that the attentions of Mutsuo Toi became unwelcome and he decided to avenge himself on those who had rejected him.

Withdrawn and isolated after the departure of his sister and now spurned in love, Mutsuo Toi took action. On the night of 20 May 1938 he cut the electricity line to the village, plunging the community into darkness. At around 1.30 a.m. the following morning he killed his 76-year-old grandmother by decapitating her with an axe. He then strapped two electric torches to his head and prowled through the village like a young man engaged in *yobai*. However, when he entered the houses of his neighbours, he did not attempt to seduce their daughters. Instead he killed them. Using an axe, a Browning shotgun and a curved, single-edged Japanese sword – commonly known as a samurai sword – he murdered 29 neighbours. Twenty-seven of them died at the

NIGHT-CRAWLING

Yobai or 'night-crawling' has long been a practice in rural Japan. A young man would visit his intended at night. They would make love and he would slip away in the morning. If the couple were to marry, parents would often turn a blind eye to this. However, once they had been 'caught', a more public courtship would be called for. But there were dangers. In the province of Fukuoka, youths would go night-crawling naked, as in that prefecture it was illegal to attack a naked intruder since he was probably a youth engaged in *yobai* rather than a thief. Young men would also urinate on the bottom of doors to stop them squeaking when they were opened.

A young man would cover his face with a cloth to avoid embarrassment if the young lady rejected his advances. Sometimes young men would travel to neighbouring villages to try their luck with girls who would not know or recognize them.

Reportedly *yobai* is still practised in remote areas. It is certainly a popular theme in Japanese pornography and there are establishments that offer *yobai* services.

scene of the attacks and two others were very badly wounded and died of their injuries later. Three more were seriously wounded, but survived. After about an hour and half, almost half of the residents of the small community were dead. At dawn, Mutsuo Toi committed suicide by shooting himself in the chest.

Mutsuo Toi's attack was not entirely unexpected. He was already regarded as a menace to society. The authorities had been informed and had revoked his gun licence. Nevertheless, he had managed to retain a shotgun and stashed away other weapons secretly.

A high sex drive

He left a series of long suicide notes explaining his actions. It seems that in May 1937 he was diagnosed with tuberculosis, then an incurable and fatal disease. Sufferers were shunned. Once they knew of his illness, the young women of the village were cold towards him and rejected his sexual advances. This left him frustrated. Like most young men he had a high sex drive, and he also believed that he was being rejected because he was hypersexual. It is clear that he was determined to take his revenge on those whom he thought despised him.

Mutsuo Toi chose the time of his attack carefully. He picked the early hours of the morning since he knew the young women who had rejected him would be at home and, probably, expecting the visit of a lover, so they would not raise the alarm if they heard a man entering the house. He also ensured it was dark by cutting off the electricity supply, so his victims would not recognize him until it was too late.

Regrets

In his final suicide note he said that he regretted that he would not be able to kill all of the people he wanted to. However, that would have involved killing some people he regarded as innocent. He also said that he killed his grandmother because he could not bear to leave her alive to face the shame and social stigma of being associated with a murderer.

SADA ABE

The seductress and murderer Sada Abe has been immortalized in literature and film since her arrest in 1936. Born in 1905 to a wealthy family, she was raped as a teenager. She became troublesome and her family sold her into a geisha house. The top geishas were trained from childhood in the arts and music. Sada became a low-class geisha whose role was to provide sex. After contracting syphilis, she became a licensed prostitute, which paid better.

After two years she quit to work as a waitress, but found she could not live on the low wages, so she became an unlicensed prostitute. She also became the mistress of several otherwise respectable men, but her lovers complained that she was insatiable.

One of them, Kinnosuke Kasahara, said: 'She was really strong, a real powerful one. Even though I am pretty jaded, she was enough to astound me. She wasn't satisfied unless we did it two, three, or four times a night. To her, it was unacceptable unless I had my hand on her private parts all night long ... At first it was great, but after a couple of weeks I got a little exhausted.'

She then asked him whether she could take a lover. He refused, so she ended the relationship.

When she was 30 she went to work in a restaurant with the aim of learning the business and opening a restaurant of her own. The owner, 42-year-old Kichizo Ishida, was a well-known womanizer. At the time Sada was the mistress of a politician, but she dropped him for Ishida. He was a skilful lover and, at last, she had found a man who could satisfy her, but she became excessively jealous of Ishida's wife.

On 9 May 1936 she saw a play in which a geisha attacked her lover with a large knife.

Two days later she pawned her clothes to buy a kitchen knife and threatened Ishida with it. Instead of being frightened, she said, 'he seemed delighted with it'.

Next time they were making love, she put the knife to the base of Ishida's penis and told him that she would make sure he never played around with other women. He laughed. During a prolonged bout of sexual intercourse, Sada began choking Ishida, and the partial asphyxiation improved his orgasm. She took to strangling him with the *obi* sash from her kimono. This turned them both on and they continued the practice even though it was causing Ishida considerable pain.

At 2 a.m. on 18 May 1936 Sada strangled Ishida in his sleep. After lying next to his dead body for a few hours, she cut off his genitals, saying later that she had done this because, as she could not take his head or body with her, she 'wanted to take the part of him that brought back to me the most vivid memories'.

When the crime was discovered, there was a panic. She checked into a hotel under a false name. There, 'I put his penis in my mouth and even tried to insert it inside me,' she said. She intended to commit suicide by jumping off a cliff holding Ishida's penis, but she was arrested first.

Sada asked to be executed but was sentenced to just six years, serving five. Even before she was convicted, a bestseller based on her interrogation and confession was published. Since then she has been the subject of novels, poems, plays, films and psychological studies. She continued giving interviews until she disappeared in 1970. In the West, she became best known as the subject of the 1976 movie, *In the Realm of the Senses*.

HOWARD UNRUH

USA, 6 September 1949

The veteran who took to the streets

German-American Howard Unruh was born in 1921 in East Camden, New Jersey. His father had left the family and he became deeply attached to his mother, Freda, who worked in a local soap factory. During his childhood, he was withdrawn and spent a lot of time reading the Bible on his own. He joined the army in the Second World War and fought in Europe. He returned with a 9mm Luger pistol and other mementos which he used to decorate his bedroom. In the basement he set up a firing range, where he practised daily.

Unruh also kept a diary in which he recorded the imagined slights he had suffered at the hands of others. His chief target was the Cohen family. When they chided him for taking a short cut through their back garden or turning his radio up too loud, his diary spoke of taking 'retaliation' against them – the word appeared 180 times.

Unruh erected a high wooden fence around the rear of his house to block out the world he hated. On the afternoon of 5 September 1949 he went to the movies in Philadelphia. When he returned home at three o'clock the following morning, he found his gate missing and concluded that it had been taken by one of his neighbours. That night he lay on his bed fully clothed and stared at the ceiling, plotting his revenge.

At 8 a.m. his mother prepared breakfast for him but he refused to eat. There was, she said, a wild look in his eyes. Suddenly he shot back his chair and ran from the room. When his mother followed, he threatened her with a heavy wrench. Terrified, she ran to a neighbour's house.

Unruh shrugged and moved on

Unruh loaded his Luger and stuffed another pistol into his pocket. At 9.20 a.m., wearing his best tropical worsted suit, the 28-year-old veteran went out on to the street. As he walked past a delivery truck parked two blocks away, he thrust his gun through the window and pulled the trigger. The driver, 33-year-old Roxy DiMarco, hurled himself back as the bullet whizzed past the steering wheel. Unruh shrugged and moved on.

Further down the street was a cobbler's shop run by 27-year-old John Pilarchik, who had known Unruh since he was a boy. Unruh shot him in the chest and walked out without a word. Next door was Clark Hoover barber's shop. Six-year-old Orris 'Brux' Smith was perched on a white hobby-horse while Hoover cut his hair.

'I'd have killed a thousand if I'd had enough bullets'

'I've got something for you, Clarkie,' said Unruh as he put the Luger to the boy's chest and pulled the trigger. Then he shot the 33-year-old barber as the boy's 42-year-old mother and 11-year-old sister looked on. Ignoring their screams, Unruh stepped quietly back out on to the sunlit street.

Unruh headed on to the drugstore owned by his hated neighbour Abe Cohen. On the way he bumped into the family's insurance agent, 45-year-old James Hutton, who said hello. Unruh's reply was two 9mm slugs – one in the head, one in the body. Unruh later told the police that he had politely asked Hutton to get out of his way, but Hutton had not moved fast enough.

The shots alerted Cohen who ran up the stairs into the stockroom above his store to warn his wife Rose, his mother Minnie and his son Charles. Sliding a fresh clip into his Luger, Unruh bounded up the stairs after him. In the stockroom, Unruh saw 38-year-old Rose Cohen as she took cover in a cupboard. Unruh put a bullet through the cupboard door. When she tumbled out Unruh put another shot through her head.

In the adjoining office, he found 62-year-old Minnie Cohen, phone in hand, dialling the police. Two shots ended the call and her life. Above, he could hear the sound of Abe Cohen who was trying to escape across the pitched porch roof. Unruh climbed out of the window and fired twice, hitting Cohen in the back. Cohen lost his grip and crashed to the pavement below. Unruh went down and put another bullet through his head, just to make sure. From the pavement, Unruh could see 12-year-old Charles Cohen on the roof, screaming hysterically. He had no quarrel with the boy and walked away.

VICTIMS

Maurice J. Abe Cohen, 39
Minnie Cohen, 62
Rose Cohen, 38
Alvin Day, 24
Thomas Hamilton, 2
Clark Hoover, 33
James Hutton, 45
Emma Matlack, 68
John Joseph Pilarchik, 27
Orris Martin Smith, 6
Helen Wilson, 37
John Wilson, 9
Helga Kautzach Zegrino, 28

Deadly accuracy

Unruh did not even know 24-year-old TV repairman Alvin Day, who was driving up the street. Unruh shot him once with deadly accuracy. Another motorist, 18-year-old Charles Petersen, had stopped to tend the dying James Hutton. Unruh fired several times, wounding Petersen in the legs.

At the end of the street a car was waiting at the traffic lights. Unruh walked over to it and shot dead the driver, 37-year-old Helen Wilson. Then he shot the passengers – Mrs Wilson's 68-year-old mother, Emma Matlack of Pennsauken, and nine-year-old John Wilson, who was fatally wounded.

With a long shot, Unruh wounded a truck driver climbing from his cab on the next block. Unruh then headed for a tavern owned by Frank Engel. The customers rushed to take cover in the rear as bullets tore through the front door. From an upstairs window Engel took a pot shot with his .38 revolver at Unruh, wounding him in the leg. Unruh took no notice and went about his murderous business.

Next Unruh walked into a tailor's shop. The tailor, Thomas Zegrino, got lucky as he was away, but in the back Unruh found his 28-year-old wife Helga. She fell to her knees and begged for her life, but it was useless. Unruh shot her twice. Two-year-old Tommy

INTERVIEW WITH A SPREE KILLER

When Unruh returned to his home to get more ammunition, the telephone rang. On the line was local newspaper reporter Philip Buxton.

'I'm a friend,' said Buxton, hoping to persuade Unruh to talk. 'I want to know what they're doing to you down there.'

Unruh thought for a moment. Then he said calmly: 'They haven't done anything to me – yet. I'm doing plenty to them.'

'How many have you killed?' was Buxton's next question.

'I don't know,' said Unruh. 'I haven't counted. Looks like a pretty good score.' Buxton then asked him the reason why he was killing people.

'I don't know,' Unruh replied. 'I can't answer that yet – I'm too busy. I'll have to talk to you later.' And he put the phone down and went back to the fray.

Tear-gas canisters were then being lobbed through the windows. The choking fumes drove Unruh downstairs. A few minutes later he laid down his weapons, opened the back door and came out with his hands up. The guns of 50 police marksmen were trained on him.

Officers scrambled forward and handcuffed him. As he was hurried off, one policeman asked him: 'What's the matter with you? Are you a psycho?'

'I'm no psycho,' said Unruh, apparently unconcerned. 'I have a good mind.'

Hamilton was watching Unruh's homicidal progress from a window. A single shot hit the child between the eyes, killing him instantly.

Then Unruh saw a small yellow house with its door slightly ajar. Inside he found a woman, Madeline Harris, and her two sons cowering in a kitchen at the back. The older boy flung himself at the gunman. Unruh loosed off two shots, one hitting the boy in the arm, the other wounding Mrs Harris in the shoulder. The younger child escaped unscathed.

Incurably insane

Unruh was now out of ammunition. As he walked home, he could hear police sirens wailing in the distance. Soon his house was surrounded. Machine-gun fire came pouring through the window, followed by tear-gas canisters. After a few minutes Unruh laid down his guns and came out with his hands up.

Unruh never stood trial. He was declared incurably insane and committed to New Jersey State Mental Hospital. He never expressed the slightest remorse for his victims. He had only one regret – that there were so few. However, his conscience was troubled by the fact that he had threatened his mother with a wrench. It was also said that he was depressed over a homosexual encounter. He died at the age of 88 in 2009.

Psychiatric experts now believe that Unruh was not insane. He did not just shoot people at random in a frenzy. He knew most of the people he killed and went about killing them according to a preconceived plan. Unruh himself believed he was not crazy. When he heard sirens, he rushed home, knowing that what he had done was illegal or wrong and it is doubtful that he would have been found insane by a court today.

CHARLES STARKWEATHER

USA, 21–29 January 1958

Natural born killer

Charles Starkweather was a lowly garbage collector in Lincoln, Nebraska. Since leaving school he had had a series of menial jobs. His bosses treated him as retarded but he was determined to move up in the world – by becoming an armed robber. On 1 December 1957 he shot and killed Robert Colvert after robbing his petrol station on the outskirts of Lincoln. He confessed to his girlfriend, Caril Fugate, about the robbery, but said someone else had killed Colvert. He knew she didn't believe him. Feeling euphoric and powerful, Starkweather stopped turning up for work and was promptly fired.

Starkweather and Fugate had been going out since she was 13, though her parents thought that he was too old for their daughter and tried persistently to put a stop to the relationship. Starkweather turned up at Fugate's house on 21 January 1958 carrying a rifle – he intended to go hunting jack-rabbits. There was an argument and he shot and killed Fugate's mother and stepfather, and killed her two-year-old half-sister with a knife. Then the couple sat down and watched TV.

That evening they wrapped up the bodies and dragged them outside. Fugate's mother's body was stuffed down an outside toilet, her half-sister's body was left in a box on top of it, while her stepfather's body was hidden in a disused chicken coop. Fugate later claimed that she was not present during the slaughter of her family, but turned up to find Starkweather with a gun and her family gone. Starkweather said that Fugate had participated in the slaughter of her family and egged him on.

'Better to be left to rot on some high hill and be remembered than to be buried alive in some stinking place'

'Sick with the Flue'

For the next week they lived as husband and wife, warning off visitors with a sign that said: 'Stay away Every Body is sick with the Flue.' However, on Saturday 25 January Fugate's sister Barbara turned up with Starkweather's best friend, Bob von Busch, and their newborn baby. Then Starkweather's brother Rodney arrived. Fugate warned them that if they did not go away her mother would get hurt. They called the police. When a patrol car turned up, Fugate repeated the story about the flu and said that her family had fallen out with von Busch and that was why he had called the cops.

More people turned up, only to be fobbed off. They too reported their concerns to the police. But before the police returned to the house Fugate and Starkweather had fled. He was carrying a hunting knife, a shotgun whose barrel he had sawn down and a .32 pistol he had found in the house. Soon after the bodies were found and the hunt was on.

Outside Bennet, a short drive southeast of Lincoln, the fugitives followed a dirt track up to the property of 72-year-old August Meyer, a family friend who used to let them hunt there. But there had been a fresh fall of snow and their car got stuck. Starkweather walked up to the farmhouse and killed the old man. They ransacked the house and found a .22 pump-action repeating rifle. Fugate did not want to stay in the house. Instead they planned to stay the night in the cyclone cellar of a derelict school nearby. On the way, they were offered a lift by 17-year-old Robert Jensen, the son of a local store-owner, and his fiancée, 16-year-old Carol King.

A gun to the back of the head

Starkweather decided that Jensen and King were just the sort of people he hated – respectable middle-class All-American kids who planned to get married once they had graduated. He put his gun to the back of Jensen's head and told him to hand over his money. At the school, Fugate stayed in the car while Starkweather took Jensen and King into the cellar at gunpoint.

Jensen died from six shots to the head. King was found with her jeans and panties around her ankles. She had been stabbed viciously several times in the genitals. Starkweather later said he had attempted to rape King, but Fugate had murdered and mutilated her out of jealousy.

Taking Jensen's car, the couple decided to return to Lincoln, only to find patrol cars outside Fugate's house. The following morning, they forced their way into the home of millionaire businessman C. Lauer Ward at gunpoint. Ward had already gone to work, but Starkweather and Fugate forced his wife Clara and their maid Lillian Fencl to wait on them. Meanwhile they heard of the discovery of the bodies of Meyer, Jensen and King on the radio.

When Ward returned home, Starkweather shot and killed him. The couple then stole some money, loaded Mrs Ward's blue Packard with tins of food from the kitchen and fled. The next morning Clara Ward and Lillian Fencl were found tied up. They had been stabbed to death.

With nine dead, Lincoln's mayor posted a $1,000 reward. A picture of Starkweather and Fugate grinning was on the front page of the evening paper. People barricaded themselves in their houses. Gun stores were packed. A hundred-strong posse gathered outside the sheriff's office. The National Guard cruised the streets in jeeps with machine guns, and a spotter plane circled over the city.

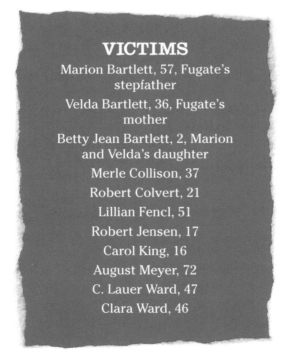

VICTIMS

Marion Bartlett, 57, Fugate's stepfather

Velda Bartlett, 36, Fugate's mother

Betty Jean Bartlett, 2, Marion and Velda's daughter

Merle Collison, 37

Robert Colvert, 21

Lillian Fencl, 51

Robert Jensen, 17

Carol King, 16

August Meyer, 72

C. Lauer Ward, 47

Clara Ward, 46

CARIL FUGATE

Born in 1943, Fugate was just 13 when she met Starkweather, although she could pass for 18. Her father was a drunkard and a peeping Tom who died in jail. Fugate seemed the perfect mate for the moody Starkweather. She was self-confident, opinionated and rebellious.

Like Starkweather, she did badly at school. Considered slow, she had little experience of life and had left Lincoln only once for a holiday in Nebraska's Sand Hill.

They enjoyed the countryside around Lincoln and drove around listening to rock 'n' roll on some distant radio station, but she tried to dump Starkweather shortly before he killed her family.

They told conflicting stories about their murderous spree, blaming each other. Starkweather appeared as the main prosecution witness at her trial and said: 'If I fry in the electric chair, then Caril should be sitting on my lap.'

The fugitives headed westwards, and the following morning they crossed the state line into Wyoming, into an area of badlands where outlaws used to hide in the days of the wild west. The couple decided they needed to change cars again but this was no problem. A short distance from Douglas, they spotted a Buick belonging to salesman Merle Collison who was asleep at the roadside. Starkweather shot him seven times.

When he tried to drive off, Starkweather found the handbrake was stuck fast. Geologist Joe Sprinkle stopped to help. Seeing the bullet holes in Collison's body, Sprinkle made a grab for Starkweather's gun. Deputy Sheriff William Romer who was driving by saw them grappling and stopped. Fugate ran over to his car, pointed at Starkweather and said: 'He just killed a man.'

'Nobody remembers a crazy man'

Starkweather ran back to Mrs Ward's Packard and roared off back towards Douglas, while Deputy Romer put out an all-points bulletin. Starkweather tore through Douglas at high speed with police in pursuit. As his speed climbed to over 100 mph, Country Sheriff Earl Heflin put a bullet through the back window of the Packard. Starkweather screeched to a halt, bleeding copiously. A piece of flying glass had nicked his ear. He thought he was bleeding to death.

Appearing before the press wearing tight jeans, a black motorcycle jacket and cowboy boots, with a cigarette dangling from his lips, Starkweather personified the teenage rebel killer. The ultimate juvenile delinquent, he became a TV celebrity, appearing on the news every night. Refusing an insanity plea, he said: 'Nobody remembers a crazy man.'

Starkweather went to the electric chair on 25 June 1959. The youngest woman ever to be tried for first-degree murder in the USA, Fugate was sentenced to life imprisonment. She was paroled in 1976. Their story was retold in the 1973 cult movie *Badlands*, starring Martin Sheen and Sissy Spacek, and was regarded as the inspiration behind Oliver Stone's *Natural Born Killers* (1994).

CHARLES WHITMAN JR

USA, 1 August 1966

Sniper in the tower

At 11.48 a.m. on 1 August 1966 17-year old Alec Hernandez was cycling across the downtown campus of the University of Texas in Austin when a .35 rifle bullet ripped through his leg. Then, out of the clear blue sky, more bullets came raining down. Three students, late for class, fell in quick succession. This was the beginning of a brief but bloody hail of fire from the tower of the university's main building.

Eighteen-year-old Claire Wilson, who was eight months pregnant, was heading across the campus to her anthropology class when a bullet hit her in the belly. She survived, but her unborn child's skull was crushed. Freshman Thomas Eckman was shot dead as he knelt beside her.

Postgraduate mathematician Robert Boyer had recently secured a teaching post and would be setting up home with his pregnant wife and two children. As he headed for an early lunch he was shot, fatally, in the back. People began to take cover and found themselves pinned down.

At 11.52 a.m., four minutes after the shooting started, the police got a call telling them that there had been some shooting at the university tower. Officers rushed to the campus. One of the first there was rookie patrolman Billy Speed. He spotted the killer on the observation deck of the 30-storey tower that overlooked the mall and took cover. The sniper shot him dead. The police replied with volleys of small-arms fire that cracked ineffectually around the top of the tower. The sniper was safe behind a low wall with drainage slits around the bottom that made perfect gun ports.

Killed instantly

Electrical repairman Roy Dell Schmidt was getting out of his truck when saw puffs of smoke coming from the tower's observation gallery. He told the man next to him that they were out of range. They weren't. Seconds later, a rifle bullet smashed into Schmidt's chest, killing him instantly.

Among the window-shoppers on Guadeloupe Street to the west of the campus was Paul Sonntag, a lifeguard at a local swimming pool. With him was his fiancée Claudia Rutt who was on her way to the doctor's for a polio shot. Suddenly Claudia sank to the ground, clutching her breast. Sonntag bent over her. The next shot took him out.

Further up the street, visiting professor Harry Walchuk was hit in the throat and collapsed dead at a news-stand. In the next block, Thomas Karr was returning to his apartment when he dropped to the pavement, dying. Basketball coach Billy Snowden stepped out of a barbershop and was wounded in the shoulder.

Outside the Rae Ann dress shop, Iraqi chemistry student Abdul Khashab, his fiancée Janet Paulos and trainee sales assistant Lana Phillips fell wounded within seconds of each other. Shop manager Homer Kelly was trying to drag them into Sheftall's jewellery store when two bullet fragments smashed into his leg. All four survived.

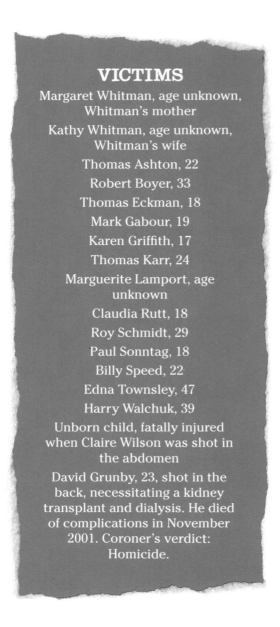

VICTIMS

Margaret Whitman, age unknown,
Whitman's mother

Kathy Whitman, age unknown,
Whitman's wife

Thomas Ashton, 22

Robert Boyer, 33

Thomas Eckman, 18

Mark Gabour, 19

Karen Griffith, 17

Thomas Karr, 24

Marguerite Lamport, age
unknown

Claudia Rutt, 18

Roy Schmidt, 29

Paul Sonntag, 18

Billy Speed, 22

Edna Townsley, 47

Harry Walchuk, 39

Unborn child, fatally injured
when Claire Wilson was shot in
the abdomen

David Grunby, 23, shot in the
back, necessitating a kidney
transplant and dialysis. He died
of complications in November
2001. Coroner's verdict:
Homicide.

To the north, two students were wounded on their way to the biology building. Beyond them, Associated Press reporter Robert Heard was hit in the shoulder. To the east, Iran-bound Peace Corps trainee Thomas Ashton was sunning himself on the roof of the Computation Center when a single round ended his life.

At 12.30 p.m., a man in combat fatigues began chipping large chunks off the observation deck with a tripod-mounted high-calibre M14. Meanwhile a Cessna light aircraft circled overhead with a police marksman on board. But the turbulent air made aiming impossible and the plane was eventually driven away when the sniper put a bullet through the fuselage.

'Cover me'

Patrolman Houston McCoy found his way through the underground passageway that connected the university buildings to the foyer of the tower. With him was 40-year-old retired USAF tailgunner Allen Crum, a civilian employee of the university who immediately deputized. Patrolman Ramiro Martinez risked his life zigzagging across the open plaza to join them. They took the lift to the top of the tower. Outside the door of the observation gallery, Crum took charge.

Carrying a rifle, Crum headed west, while Martinez, with a .38 service revolver, headed eastwards around the gallery, followed by McCoy carrying a shotgun. From the north side of the walkway, Martinez saw the gunman a short distance away lying in wait for Crum. When the veteran Crum loosed off a shot, tearing a great chunk out of the parapet, the gunman turned and ran back into the sights of Martinez, who fired – and missed. The gunman returned fire but the bullet screamed harmlessly over the officer's head. Martinez then emptied his remaining five rounds into the gunman. McCoy blasted him twice with the shotgun. The gunman hit the concrete still holding his weapon. He was still moving. Martinez grabbed the shotgun, ran forward and shot the gunman at point-blank range in the head.

THE MAKING OF A KILLER

Born in 1941 at Lake Worth, Florida, Charles Whitman Jr was an exemplary son. At 12 he became an Eagle Scout, one of the youngest ever. His father was a fanatic about guns and raised his son knowing how to handle them. He also beat the boy. By the time Whitman enlisted in the US Marines in 1959 he was an expert marksman. Despite several breaches of discipline, he won a Marine Corps scholarship to the University of Texas. After years of beatings and abuse, his mother left his father and moved to Austin to be near her son. By then Whitman had begun beating his own wife, Kathy, though he was full of remorse. He quit the Marines and enrolled himself on more courses, overloading himself with work. The fees also put him under financial pressure.

He sought help from the university's psychiatrist, saying that he was 'thinking about going up on the tower with a deer rifle and to start shooting people'. On the night before the shooting, he wrote a note saying that he intended to kill his wife. 'I cannot rationally pinpoint any specific reason for doing this. I don't know whether this is selfishness, or if I don't want to have to face the embarrassment my actions would surely cause her,' he said, adding that he intended to kill his mother for the same reason.

Having killed them, he set off for the university with three rifles, a sawn-off shotgun, two pistols, three knives, a machete, 700 rounds of ammunition, enough canned food for several days, a five-gallon bottle of distilled water, Dexedrine tablets, sunglasses, a compass, an alarm clock, a lantern, toilet paper, a spray deodorant and a green towel. Plainly he was expecting a long siege.

Reaching the observation deck, he was met by the receptionist, 47-year-old Edna Townsley, who was working on her day off. He clubbed her with the butt of his rifle and finished her off with a bullet to the head. Then the Gabour family from Texarkana turned up. Whitman shot them as well. Nineteen-year-old Mark Gabour and his aunt Marguerite Lamport were killed; his mother Mary and his younger brother Michael were injured. Whitman then turned his gun on the mall below and began shooting anyone who came into his sights.

Once the sniper was dead, the police established his identity. He was 25-year-old ex-Marine Charles Whitman Jr. At his home in Jewell Street, ten minutes' drive from the University of Texas, they found the naked body of his wife Kathy. She had been stabbed three times in the chest with a hunting knife early that morning. With her was a note that said: '3 a.m. Wife and mother both dead.'

At Whitman's mother's apartment in Guadeloupe Street, they found the body of Margaret Whitman. She had put up a fight. Her fingers were broken where they had been slammed in a door with such force that her engagement ring had been driven into her flesh. She had been stabbed in the chest and shot in the back of the head.

A handwritten note by the body read: 'To whom it may concern, I have just taken my mother's life. I am very upset over having done it. However, I feel that if there is a heaven she is definitely there now. And if there is no life after, I have relieved her of suffering here on earth … I am truly sorry that this is the only way I could see to relieve her sufferings but I think it was best. Let there be no doubt in your mind I loved that woman with all my heart. If there exists a God let him understand my actions and judge me accordingly.'

FRANK KULAK

USA, 14 April 1969

Bomber turned gunman

Like Howard Unruh, Frank Kulak was a veteran of the Second World War. Again like Unruh, he was a big man and a good soldier. At 16 he lied about his age to enlist in the US Marines. As an explosives expert, he saw action against the Japanese in the bitter fighting on Okinawa, the final and bloodiest battle of the Pacific War. After the war he was demobilized, but in 1950 he re-enlisted to fight the communists in Korea, where he won a Purple Heart. Then he was invalided out. His unit had been shelled and he had lost three fingers on his left hand. But he was, perhaps, more seriously scarred mentally by the fighting he had been through.

When Kulak returned to his home in Chicago's South Side in 1952, his missing fingers made it difficult for him to find work. Poor and idle, he became embittered and gradually soured into the neighbourhood oddball who yelled at the local children and made them cry. He never married and lived with his sister in a seven-room apartment on the third floor of a large house at 9521 South Exchange Avenue. Spending his days brooding in the apartment, he was constantly reliving the nightmares of combat. 'He was always talking about the war,' recalled Susan Kulak, a niece who was 19 when her uncle finally went off the rails. 'He was always talking about the Japs.'

Kulak might have remained an embittered old grouch if it had not been for the Vietnam War. After the war in Korea had been fought to a standstill in July 1953, the principal confrontation between the communist world and the West moved to Vietnam, which also found itself divided into a communist North and a supposedly democratic South. In March 1965, to support the increasingly beleaguered South, the USA sent in ground troops. Although American troops won the major engagements, the Vietnamese resorted to guerrilla tactics, tying down larger forces and leading to what would become, for both sides, a long and terrible struggle.

Demos and draft dodgers

Back home in the USA there was growing opposition to the war, especially among young people who were expected to go and fight it. Thousands turned out for demonstrations. Others dodged the draft by fleeing to Canada. In January 1968 the communists launched the Tet offensive, attacking over 100 towns and cities in South Vietnam and seizing the compound of the US Embassy in the capital, Saigon. This demonstrated to most Americans that the war was unwinnable, but it was four more years before the administration of Richard Nixon managed to negotiate a US withdrawal.

Vietnam was the world's first truly televisual war. Night after night, TV news showed footage of the fighting. For Kulak, the ugly memories of war were being made terribly real again. There was no way he could block it out. As the war dragged on it filled the newspapers and magazines, as well as the nightly news and everyone's conversation. It pushed him over the edge. By 1968 the war had divided the country. The peace movement brought out thousands of demonstrators, while those who supported the war felt that if they did not stop the communists in Vietnam they would have to fight them in their own backyard.

In his own warped way Kulak sought to bring the reality of war home to the American public. He began making bombs and setting them off around the neighbourhood. On 12 April 1968 30-year-old Edward Cummings was killed when he picked up one of Kulak's bombs near the South Side highway and it exploded. Another four people were injured on 4 July 1968 when they picked up a bomb in a park. Then he bombed the toy department of the Goldblatt Brothers' department store because it was selling toy guns and war games. Sixty-five-year-old Kathrun O. Lebeter was killed.

The Chicago bomb-squad's investigation led them to Kulak. When 40-year-old Detective Jerome A. Stubig and 48-year-old Sergeant James Schaffer arrived at Kulak's apartment he was ready for them. Inside he had an M1 rifle, two carbines, two 12-bore shotguns, two automatic pistols, 2,000 rounds of ammunition, hand grenades and a grenade launcher, 10 kilograms of gunpowder and chemical explosives, along with a lethal assortment of home-made bombs, pipes, cylinders and military fuses.

SIX HOURS IN THE LIFE OF FRANK KULAK

In November 1969, just seven months after Kulak's arrest, an experimental theatre group from Cali in Colombia put on a play called *Six Hours in the Life of Frank Kulak* at the Teatro Colon in Bogotá. Written by Enrique Buenaventura, it was based on an article in the *Chicago Tribune* of 15 April 1969, contrasting the article with the story of Van Trei, who was captured and later executed after attempting to mine a bridge in South Vietnam shortly before US Defense Secretary Robert McNamara passed over it. McNamara was thought to be the architect of the Vietnam war, though he later changed his mind about its wisdom. Kulak's breakdown and Van Trei's arrest were performed simultaneously, and the curtain falls with a reading of the *Chicago Tribune* article and Vietnamese peasants chanting: 'We are with Van Trei.'

Back in a foxhole

In Kulak's eyes the knock on the door meant the enemy was now massing for attack. The ex-Marine reacted as if he were back in a foxhole, and he knew how to deal with this situation. He tossed a grenade out of the window. The two officers were standing on the wooden stairs that led up to the third floor. The staircase was blown apart and the two men fell over two floors to the ground. Then Kulak emptied his carbine into their twisted bodies. Satisfied they were dead, he prepared for a fresh assault, setting up weapons at each window of the apartment. Then he began heaving bombs at the street below and firing randomly at pedestrians, who ran for cover.

MICHAEL CLARK

In the USA the phenomenon of spree killing became popularly associated with the Vietnam war, partly because Charles Whitman, the sniper in the tower, was an ex-Marine, though he had not served overseas. However, the year before Whitman devastated Austin, there was a spree killing that seemed to have nothing to do with the war. On 8 May 1965 16-year-old Sea Scout Michael Clark of Long Beach, California, took the family's Cadillac and drove off for a rendezvous with mass murder. With him he had his father's Swedish Mauser deer rifle with a four-power telescopic sight and several dozen armour-piercing bullets. Skirting Los Angeles, he headed north on Route 101 until he collided with a crash barrier near Santa Maria. Abandoning the car, he climbed to the top of a hill near the highway.

At around 6 a.m. he fired his first shot at the driver of one of the cars below – and missed. After a second bullet hit his front fender, the driver sped off to alert the police. Shortly after, William Reida, with his wife and four small children, drove into Clark's sights. Bullets hit both Reida and his five-year-old son Kevin, killing him. The car veered off the road. Mrs Reida waved down passing motorists. Two stopped, but both drivers were shot dead before they could get out.

Two more passing motorists were hit, though not fatally, and six more were wounded by flying glass. The police arrived. Clark held them off for over two hours, wounding one officer in the arm. At around 8.30 a.m., as they closed in, Clark turned the rifle on himself and blew his brains out. No one had any explanation why a model son had turned into a cold-blooded killer.

The five other tenants in the building cowered in the basement and, at the Sacred Heart Parochial School across the road, children huddled under their desks. The police sent back-up and Kulak was soon trading fire with over 100 officers. Trained sharpshooters were brought in but the seasoned veteran was too good for them. They could not pin him down.

The police used bullhorns to beg Kulak to lay down his weapons. Kulak's 51-year-old brother Harold shouted up: 'Frank, Frank, this isn't a war zone. The war is over. We have a Marine ambulance here for you.' Katherine Potts, Kulak's sister, made a similar appeal. It was answered with another rifle shot.

The siege continued for six hours. Eventually the police stopped firing. They had sent a small squad of men to creep into the building. From a position out of the line of fire on the floor below Deputy Superintendent James Rochford managed to talk to the gunman. At 8.45 p.m., after three hours of negotiation, Kulak showed himself at the back window. Instantly 100 guns were trained on his head and chest. He stood there for a while. Then he sat down on the window-sill, slowly running his disfigured hand through his Marine-style crew-cut and began to cry. Twenty minutes later he surrendered. Four people were dead, 20 wounded.

The next day, his 42nd birthday, Frank Kulak was arraigned on four murder charges. He admitted the bombings, saying he wanted to bring home to people 'how horrible war is'. Kulak was subsequently found unfit to stand trial and the 'Mad Bomber' was finally sent to a psychiatric facility at Chester jail in Illinois.

MARK ESSEX

USA, 31 December 1972 –
7 January 1973

'The Battle of New Orleans'

During the campaign for black civil rights in the 1960s and 1970s, 23-year-old African-American Mark Essex singlehandedly embarked on an armed struggle. He had been born and brought up in the quiet midwestern town of Emporia, Kansas, where racism, if not unknown, did not reach the vilest excesses of the southern states or the urban ghettos. However, to avoid being drafted into the army and sent to Vietnam, Essex joined the US Navy where he suffered a level of racism he was unprepared for. After being discharged from the service, he began a war against the white world.

It began with an attack on a police station on New Year's Eve 1972. His first victim was, ironically, a 19-year-old black police cadet, Alfred Harrell. He was unarmed. Lieutenant Horace Perez, a white officer, was also injured. As Essex made his escape, he shot Officer Edwin Hosli in the back. Hosli never recovered from the wound and died in hospital two months later.

Essex suffered a flesh wound in the attack and the police followed the trail of blood and spent shells, which led them to a church in the nearby ghetto of Gert Town. Fearing that any attack on the church might spark a full-scale race riot, Chief of Police Clarence Giarrusso pulled his men back and Essex escaped.

At 6 p.m. on 2 January Essex walked into Joe's Grocery Store on the corner of Erato Street and South Gayoso not far from the church. He had a bloody bandage around his left hand. Store owner Joseph Perniciaro reported this to the police. Another tip-off led them back to the church where they found fresh blood, bullets and a note from Essex to the pastor, apologizing for breaking in. But there was no sign of Essex himself.

'The revolution's here'

At 10.15 a.m. on 7 January Essex returned to Perniciaro's shop and shot him in the chest. Out in the street, Essex stuck his rifle in through the window of a 1968 Chevrolet and ordered the driver Marvin Albert to get out. Albert had served in Vietnam and was unfazed.

'Are you crazy?' he said. 'I don't want to kill you,' said Essex. 'I'm just killing honkies today, but I will kill you, too.'

Realizing the gunman was deadly serious, Albert got out. Essex leapt into the car and made his getaway. Later the stolen car was found in the garage of the downtown Howard Johnson Hotel on Loyola Avenue.

An hour after the shooting of Perniciaro, three black housekeepers in the hotel bumped into a man with a rifle on the 18th floor. 'Don't worry,' he said. 'We're not going to shoot any blacks, just whites. The revolution's here.'

Twenty-seven-year-old Dr Robert Steagall and his wife Betty were leaving their room to check out. Essex shot Steagall in the chest. Betty fell to her knees by her husband's body. Essex put the muzzle of his .44 carbine to her head and pulled the trigger. He dropped a red, green and black Pan-African flag beside them and then set fire to their room.

The hotel switchboard began getting reports of an armed man roaming the hotel, shooting guests. Assistant manager Frank Schneider went to investigate. When he came out of the lift on the 11th floor, Essex shot him in the head. General manager Walter Collins was also on the case. Essex shot him too. He died in hospital three weeks later.

On the eighth floor, Essex found 43-year-old San Francisco broadcast executive Robert Beamish standing by the pool and shot him in the stomach. He fell into the pool and pretended to be dead. Air trapped inside his coat kept Beamish afloat until he was rescued two hours later.

Essex started more fires and shot at the firefighters when they turned up, wounding Fire Lieutenant Tim Ursin who lost most of his left arm. A policeman following Ursin up the ladder returned fire. Other armed officers took up positions on surrounding high buildings. Meanwhile Essex fired at the policemen, firefighters and spectators on the street below. He hit Officer Ken Solis and Sergeant Emanuel Palmisano. Bullets to the head killed Officers Philip Coleman and Paul Persigo on the spot. An ambulance driver and a civil defence fire chief who had turned up to see if he could help were wounded. Deputy Police Superintendent Louis Sirgo led a search party through the hotel. On the 16th floor Essex shot him in the spine, fatally wounding him.

Live on TV

Downtown New Orleans became a city under siege. The police had had two tense confrontations with local black militants in the past two years. With the casualties they were taking, they assumed they were facing a well-armed band of urban guerrillas.

BLACK POWER

Mark Essex drew inspiration from the Black Power movement. It was begun in 1966 by civil rights activist Stokely Carmichael, who had already told Martin Luther King that he was 'not for that non-violent stuff' any more. He urged African-American troops to return from Vietnam 'and fight here because here is where the fight is'. By April 1967 he was telling African-Americans: 'If a white man tries to walk over you, kill him … One match and you can retaliate … Burn, baby, burn.' He later explained that the call for black power was 'the last reasonable opportunity for this society to work out its racial problems short of prolonged destructive guerrilla warfare'.

The Black Panther Party, which started in 1966 as a black community-protection group in Oakland, California, heeded the cry and called for the arming of all blacks. This led to shootouts with the police in California, New York and Chicago. In 1968 leader Huey P. Newton was convicted of the manslaughter of a police officer.

Black Muslim Malcolm X also advocated the use of violence. In his famous 'Ballot or Bullet' speech in 1964 he said: 'I'm non-violent with those who are non-violent with me. But when you drop that violence on me, then you've made me go insane, and I'm not responsible for what I do. And that's the way every Negro should get.'

NAVY CAREER

As a medical orderly in the navy, Essex was put on report for playing loud music – although whites did the same without punishment. When his boss, a white dentist, claimed that the charge was racially motivated, Essex became the target of constant harassment. He was disciplined for the tiniest infraction. Then, when a white petty officer made a remark about Essex 'smiling and shuffling', Essex instantly took it as a racist slur, leapt on the officer and began beating him with his fists in a rage. It was the first time that Essex had ever hit a white man.

Eventually, Essex went absent without leave but was persuaded to turn himself in. At his court martial, Essex explained that he had begun to hate all white people: 'I was tired of going to whites and telling them my problems and not getting anything done about it'. He was confined to barracks for 30 days. A few weeks later, he was discharged from the service for a 'character disorder'.

After that, he began associating with Black Muslims and Black Power groups. In his spare time he began studying his African heritage and took the name 'Mata', the Swahili for 'bow'.

The gunfire was now coming from a concrete structure on the roof which covered the top of the stairwell. As the police returned fire using grenades, mortars, rockets and even 20mm cannons, people across America watched a spree killer in action, live, for the first time in what the media were calling the 'Battle of New Orleans'. The police tried using tear gas but it drifted away in the wind. The Marine Corps sent in an armour-plated CH-46 helicopter. Carrying a squad of police marksmen, the helicopter swooped past the hotel ten times as they fired hundreds of glowing tracer bullets into the lengthening shadows. But as the helicopter veered away, police and newsmen in adjacent buildings heard cries from the roof: 'I'm still here. Come and get me, you motherfucking pigs. Power to the people.'

At 9.25 p.m. the helicopter flew past again. This time Essex bolted into the open and fired at the helicopter's transmission. In the withering crossfire that ensued he was hit more than 200 times. 'We've got one of them,' was the message sent out on police radio. But in the dark it was impossible to tell whether Essex was alone. The police waited out the long hours of the night. Only the following afternoon did they make their final assault on the roof. A five-hour search of the hotel uncovered nothing but three suitcases of .44 Magnum ammunition. Chief Giarrusso said: 'Either there was only one, or another got away.'

Louisiana Attorney General William Guste maintained that the shooting was part of a black conspiracy. Essex's mother maintained that he had acted alone from private motivation. 'It all started in the Navy,' she said. 'He was alright when he left.' However, that Essex's motivation was political is clear. After the murder of two black students during a campus demonstration on 16 November 1972, he wrote to his mother: 'I have now decided that the white man is my enemy. I will fight to regain my manhood or die trying.' And after Essex was dead the police broke into his apartment and found the walls daubed with revolutionary slogans.

ROBERT POULIN

Canada, 27 October 1975

The quiet Canadian

At 1 p.m. on the afternoon of 27 October 1975 the Ottawa fire department were called to a routine domestic fire. Two fire trucks arrived outside 5 Warrington Drive in a quiet suburban area of Ottawa, where they were met by Mrs Mary Poulin who had called them. Black smoke was issuing from the basement where her teenage son Robert lived. Two firefighters donned oxygen masks and made their way down the stairs. The smoke was so thick that they had to feel their way. But even through the breathing apparatus they noticed an unpleasant smell, like burning meat.

In the basement bedroom they found the charred body of a girl spread-eagled on what remained of the bed. She was naked except for a bloodstained blouse. Her head was covered with a plastic bag. The police were called. After the fire had been put out, detectives began their investigation. The dead girl's wrists had been handcuffed to the bed-head. Ski bindings had secured her feet to the foot of the bed. It was clear she had been raped. The bloodstains on the remnants of her blouse revealed that she been stabbed to death.

A trail of half-charred pornographic magazines up the stairs had been doused with paraffin and set alight. Plainly the arsonist had wanted to burn the whole house down, but the tiny bedroom window had been left shut. Starved of oxygen, the fire had snuffed itself out.

Prime suspect

The prime suspect was the occupant of the bedroom, 18-year-old Robert Poulin. Poulin came from a military family. His father had been an air force pilot. Earlier that year Poulin had applied for officer training in the Campbell Highlanders militia. After an hour-long interview, he had every reason to believe he had been accepted. But the three-man board had decided that he was too immature. Instead, he joined the militia as a private. Two weeks before the murder of the girl, he dropped out of training. He had lied about his interest in school sports and had been found out. It was the final blow. He went to a local store with the last of his savings and paid $109 for a Winchester shotgun. Then, in his lonely basement, he sawed off the barrel.

'The day I would kill myself would be a Sunday, for if I was going to die, the people that made up my family were going to suffer'

Mrs Poulin said she had seen him on the morning of the fire and knew he was due to attend a theology class at the St Pius X High School at 2 p.m. That day Father Robert Bedard was giving a talk on Christ and the problems of modern society in classroom 71.

POULIN'S DIARY

On 7 April 1975 Robert Poulin spelled out his intentions. He had just flunked a biology test. 'For the last couple of weeks,' his diary entry read, 'I have been fairly depressed … thought of committing suicide, but I don't want to die before I have had the pleasure of fucking some girl. So I decided to order a model gun from an ad in *Gallery* magazine. With this I was going to threaten a girl in one of the dark streets around here and rape her. I planned to carry my father's scout knife strapped to the inside of my right leg. If the girl caused me any trouble I would kill her, for I was planning to kill myself anyhow, and I have nothing to lose. After that, I would wait for a reason for killing myself.'

On another occasion he had written of taking his father's rifle and killing his whole family, but then decided against it as 'death is pure bliss and I would not want them to be happy'. Instead he planned to douse the contents of the house with petrol and set it alight before shooting himself. He even planned to burn the place down soon after his parents' pay-day so that they would lose the largest possible amount of money.

At about 2.30 p.m. he was halfway through his talk when the classroom door creaked slowly open. The students at the back glanced around and saw a foot edge around the door. It was followed by the barrel of a shotgun. The young man carrying it, judging from his smiling face, was in some kind of a trance. Then he began to fire.

The room filled with screams. Father Bedard hurled himself to the floor, urging his students to do likewise. For some, it was already too late. After about two minutes the firing stopped. The deathly silence that followed was punctuated by the sound of one more shot. It came from outside the classroom.

Dead teenagers

Then panic erupted. Some students smashed the classroom windows and flung themselves out. However, Father Bedard remained composed. He got up and walked cautiously over to the classroom door and opened it. Outside, the gunman lay dead on the floor. He had turned the gun on himself and half his face was blown away. The sawn-off Winchester lay beside him. The body was that of a mere teenager. Despite the boy's appalling self-inflicted disfigurement, Father Bedard recognized him as one of his students: Robert Poulin.

While Poulin had died instantly when the shotgun cartridge blew off the top of his head, 17-year-old Mark Hough suffered fatal wounds to the back of the head and neck and died in hospital four days later. Six other students were wounded. Barclay Holbrook suffered damage to the lung, and Mark Potvin and Terry Handenberg also had neck wounds. Three students were discharged almost immediately.

Mrs Poulin and her husband Stuart feared that the dead girl in their basement was one of their three daughters, but all three were later found safe and the identity of the victim remained a mystery. Robert Poulin did not have a girlfriend, but one of Poulin's sisters said that he was interested in a 17-year-old Sri Lankan girl named Kim Rabot, who lived nearby.

THE MIND OF KILLER

Born in 1957, Robert Poulin was described as a 'strange, quiet boy'. At school he was conscientious and hardworking. When he was 12 his third sister, Jody, was born and Poulin moved into the basement where he lived out a secret life, alone. He played war games and plastered the walls with pictures of naked women, torn from the soft-porn magazines that were stacked on the floor. His diaries and notebooks revealed that he was desperately lonely, yearning for sexual contact and deeply tormented by his inability to talk to girls.

Among his possessions the police found a box containing women's bras, panties, negligées, a vibrator and four pairs of handcuffs. Some of his pornographic books showed women tied up and handcuffed to bedposts.

One notebook contained the details of 18 girls. When questioned, none of them knew him, but some had received 'heavy breather' phone calls. There had also been a number of sexual assaults and attempted rapes in the area.

Poulin's diary related that he had found an ad for 'Everything' Dolls in *Playboy* magazine and sent off $29.95. 'Now I no longer think that I will have to rape a girl,' he wrote, 'and I am unsure whether or not I will still commit suicide.' However, on 5 May 1975 he noted that the 'Everything' Doll had arrived but that it was a 'big disappointment'.

In early October, in desperation, Poulin ran a small ad in the *Ottawa Journal*, which read: 'Male, 18, looking for companionship. PO Box 4021.' He received three replies – all from homosexuals. In reply to one, he wrote: 'I have never had a homosexual experience, though the thought has crossed my mind before. However, I'm not only interested in sex but in sharing other pastimes and hobbies. My favourite hobbies are, in order: war-gaming, reading (science fiction) and collecting (a variety of things, including stamps and models). I hope you have the same sort of hobbies, especially war-gaming.'

He never posted the letter.

Kim's 13-year-old brother John had been with her at the bus stop on their way to school at 8.30 that morning when Robert Poulin had approached them. Poulin had told Kim that he had something to show her and she agreed to go with him. It seems that Poulin had taken her to his basement room where he threatened her with the shotgun. He forced her to strip and handcuffed her to the bed. Then he raped her. At one point he untied her feet and released one wrist to turn her over and sodomized her. Then he had stabbed her 14 times with a hunting knife.

When Mrs Poulin had gone downstairs to the basement at around 10 a.m., the curtains that closed off Poulin's bedroom were drawn shut.

Later he came upstairs and asked her to make him a peanut-butter sandwich. After she left for her work as a lunch supervisor at a local school, he had returned to the basement. He put his 12-bore shotgun in a blue duffel bag, strapped his hunting knife across his chest and set the room on fire. Then he cycled across town to school.

Instead of going straight into class, he went to the school cafeteria, carrying the duffel bag. A witness said he looked 'scared'. Shortly before 2.30 p.m. he crossed the hall, pulled out the gun and, like a sleepwalker, turned the handle of a classroom door and slowly pushed it open with his foot.

FREDERICK COWAN

USA, 14 February 1977

The white supremacist

Thirty-three-year-old bodybuilder Frederick Cowan liked to wear an Afrika Korps hat around his home town of New Rochelle, New York. His burly body and massive biceps were covered in Nazi tattoos – an iron cross, a death's head and the double lightning bolts of the SS. Behind the lace curtains of his attic bedroom was a collection of Second World War vintage German guns. On the wall was a poster of Hitler and a swastika flag. Cowan himself had served with the US Army in Germany, but had been discharged after single-handedly turning over a Volkswagen and smashing up the car with his bare hands.

He read Nazi propaganda and wrote in a notebook: 'Nothing is lower than black and Jewish people except the police who protect them.' Few of his fellow employees at the Neptune World Wide Moving Company, where he worked as a trucker's assistant, knew of his Nazi sympathies. But after a few beers with his buddies in the Galway Bay bar, he insisted on being called 'Reinhard', after SS General Reinhard Heydrich who masterminded the 'Final Solution' – the extermination of Europe's Jews. When drunk he would mumble: 'Fuck the Jews, fuck the niggers.'

SS insignia

Cowan's Götterdämmerung fell on St Valentine's Day. Three weeks before, his supervisor, 31-year-old Norman Bing, who was Jewish, had suspended him for refusing to move a refrigerator for a customer. Cowan woke early on 14 February and donned a pair of khaki slacks, a beret with the SS 'death's head' insignia on the front and a US Army field jacket with, under it, a T-shirt with the words 'White Power' emblazoned across the front. Tucked inside his belt was a long hunting knife. He wore two .45-calibre automatic handguns and two other 9mm automatics, all fully loaded, in double shoulder holsters as he walked down to his red Pontiac GTO.

'I should have been born forty years ago, so I could have been in the SS'

On the front seat, he dispersed hundreds of rounds of .45-calibre and 9mm ammunition, along with 7.62mm rifle cartridges in bandoliers. There were rifles in the boot.

Cowan arrived at the Neptune parking lot at 7.45 a.m., just as the morning shift was clocking in. He was looking for Bing. As he barged into the main building, he bumped into three African-American employees – 60-year-old packer Joseph Hicks, 55-year-old Fred Holmes and 45-year-old James Green. Cowan shot Hicks and Holmes in the chest. Green ran off down the hall. Cowan downed him with a bullet in the back.

THE NATIONAL STATES' RIGHTS PARTY

Inside the killer's pocket the police found a membership card for the National States' Rights Party in the name of Frederick W. Cowan. On the reverse side of the card it listed several membership principles. They included: 'A free white America, Racial Separation, Expulsion of All Jews and Confiscation of ill-gotten Jewish Wealth.' And on the bottom of this same card, the party's slogan read 'Honor, Pride, Fight – Save the White.'

The party's leader, Jesse Benjamin 'J.B.' Stoner, blamed the Federal authorities for the shootout. He told *Newsweek* magazine: 'The FBI caused niggers to start harassing Cowan on the job. Apparently, the FBI's to blame for the whole thing.'

Cowan was also wearing a belt buckle inscribed, prophetically: 'I will give up my gun when they pry my cold dead fingers from around it' – the slogan of the National Rifle Association.

Next he shot 24-year-old Joseph Russo in the dispatcher's office. Russo would die from his wounds six weeks later. As Cowan burst into the cafeteria, employees scattered. He came across his friend Ronald Cowell near the exit, put a gun to his head and said: 'Go home and tell my mother not to come down to Neptune.' He didn't look back.

'Where's Norman?' bellowed Cowan. 'I'm gonna blow him away.' Then he loosed off more shots into the walls and furniture. 'People were screaming and everyone was either seeking shelter or bolting out the doors,' said employee Howard Schofield. 'When I saw bodies on the floor in the office, I ducked under a desk with another worker. We cowered there expecting the worst.'

Near the stairwell, Cowan saw 32-year-old electrician Pariyarathu Varghese, who had recently come from India to get married and had only been working at Neptune for two weeks. Cowan shot him. Varghese died on the spot.

When Bing heard the shooting, he knew Cowan was after him. He ran from his office and took cover under a wooden desk where Cowan failed to spot him. He was too busy bandaging a cut hand. Cowan then continued on his way, firing indiscriminately into the offices. Finally he took refuge in the second-floor office of the company's vice president, Richard Kirschenbaum, which had tinted windows.

At 7.55 a.m. the first patrol car arrived at the depot. Officer Allen McLeod, a 33-year-old father of two, got out, his hand resting on the butt of his .357 Magnum which was still in its holster. Cowan leashed off a burst of automatic fire, hitting McLeod in the head and chest and killing him instantly. Cowan then continued to pump fresh rounds into McLeod's dead body.

More squad cars sped to the scene. Officer Ray Satiro, a Vietnam veteran, ran to tend McLeod, but was forced to retreat with a bullet in his leg. Lieutenant Vincent Fontanarosa crashed into a parked car as 11 bullets peppered his police cruiser. Fontanarosa was hit in the shoulder, but still managed to return fire. Over 100 rounds were fired during the first few minutes of battle.

As more than 300 local policemen and FBI agents arrived to surround the warehouse, they were met by fleeing employees. Some of them were thrown to the

COWAN'S HOME ARSENAL

When he was killed, Cowan was holding two .45-calibre automatic pistols. There was a 9mm automatic on the desk along with several ammunition clips for his SACO semi-automatic assault rifle and military-style ammunition pouches. The rifle itself was leaning against an office chair next to the corpse. The other 9mm was still in its holster with blood dripping from its handle. Various ammunition clips were strewn about the office floor along with dozens of expended rifle shells.

When the police searched Cowan's attic apartment in Woodbury Street, New Rochelle, they found an astonishing arsenal: 11 cans of gunpowder, shotgun shells, primers, three antique muskets, one rifle, shell casings and equipment to make bullets, thousands of rounds of ammunition, one machete, at least 20 knives, eight Nazi bayonets and military helmets from the Second World War.

The police also found five posters of Adolf Hitler, dozens of Nazi books and many SS items, flags and belt buckles. Detective Robert Harris was shocked. 'I didn't know Fred,' he said, 'but his family were very nice people. I didn't know how a person could go that way, have such negative feelings about Jewish people and blacks.'

According to friends and relatives, Cowan had been a bright boy and a good student at the local Catholic parochial school. He only went bad after a hitch in the US Army, when he was stationed in Germany. 'I don't remember him collecting the Nazi propaganda until then,' said his brother James. 'We never expected this. We thought it was just a hobby.'

The Neptune World Wide Moving Company seems to have been blissfully unaware of Cowan's spare-time activities. Under 'psychiatric disorders' in his company medical report, it simply says: 'No'.

ground at gunpoint by policemen fearful that the gunman was escaping. Other employees locked themselves in bathrooms and closets. Snipers got into position on rooftops across the road, but could not see the gunman in his second-floor eyrie due to the tinted glass. Meanwhile Cowan opened fired on the ambulances that were arriving from all over Westchester County.

A hastily assembled search-and-rescue team went in to clear the ground floor. They shipped out the dead and wounded, and found Norman Bing alive and unharmed. Despite the danger, crowds flocked to watch. At 12.13 p.m. the police received a call from Cowan. He was hungry. He wanted potato salad and hot chocolate. 'I get very mean when I'm hungry,' he explained. After placing his order, he put the phone down.

Pool of blood

Cowan's parents were brought to the scene in an attempt to talk him out. 'Pray for Freddie,' said a distraught Mrs Cowan. 'He's gone crazy.' Then, at 2.23 p.m., police heard a muffled shot from inside the building. A few minutes later an assault team went in. They found Cowan lying face down in a pool of blood. He had a .45 pistol in each hand and a hole in his head. After killing six people and wounding four more, he had joined his idol Adolf Hitler in suicide.

BRENDA SPENCER

USA, 29 January 1979

'I don't like Mondays'

Sixteen-year-old Brenda Spencer achieved some spurious fame from her killing spree. Bob Geldof and his Irish punk band the Boomtown Rats had a UK number one hit with their song about her called 'I Don't Like Mondays'. The title came from an interview Spencer had done with the *San Diego Tribune* during the seven-hour siege at her home in San Diego, California. When asked why she had started shooting, Spencer said: 'I just did it for the fun of it. I don't like Mondays. This livens up the day. I just wanted to. It just popped into my head about last Wednesday, I think. I have to go now. I shot a pig, I think, and I want to shoot more.'

Earlier she had told a schoolmate that she wanted to 'blow a police officer's head off'. Another of Brenda's classmate said: 'She was always talking about guns, bragging about the guns her father had … She said she and her father had enough ammunition in the house for a small army. Most of the boys and girls don't like her and won't go over to her house.'

Spencer also began telling her classmates that she was going to 'do something big to get on TV'. In her perverted quest for fame, she succeeded in that at least.

Sniper fantasies

The year before Brenda Spencer resolved her inner conflicts with a gun, her parents had divorced. She remained with her father, a hunting enthusiast. Neighbours said she was a shy tomboy who was 'really quiet, and unhappy that her mother wasn't around'. She played truant from school, took drugs and committed petty thefts. In her spare time she liked watching violent videos, enjoyed shooting birds and had had 'fantasies in the past about being a sniper', a family member said. She even shot out the windows of the Grover Cleveland Elementary School across the street from her father's house with an airgun. Even so, for Christmas her father bought her a .22 semi-automatic rifle and 500 rounds of ammunition.

> 'I am having too much fun to surrender … It was just like shooting ducks in a pond'

Early in the New Year Spencer began to make plans. She moved her weapons into the garage and dug a hide-out in the garden. Then on Monday 29 January she positioned herself in a window a short distance away as children arrived at Grover Cleveland Elementary, and started shooting. The children thought that the noise they heard was a cap gun, but Principal Burton Wragg recognized the sound of real bullets and yelled: 'Go! Go! Go!'

Principal Wragg fell, hit by a bullet. School janitor Michael Suchar ran to his aid. He was also killed. The first policeman to arrive on the scene, 30-year-old Robert Robb,

WOMEN WHO KILL

Brenda Spencer was not the only female spree killer. On 30 October 1985 Sylvia Seegrist opened fire with a rifle in a shopping mall in Springfield, Pennsylvania, killing three – two men and a two-year-old – and injuring seven others. Ten years earlier she had been diagnosed with paranoid schizophrenia and had been committed and discharged several times. Asked why she had done it, she said: 'My family makes me nervous.' She was found guilty, but insane, and was given three life sentences for the murders, and seven consecutive 10-year sentences for the attempted murder of the people she had wounded.

On 20 May 1988 divorcee Laurie Dann picked up two children she had formerly babysat for in Winnetka, Illinois, to take them for an outing. Instead she drove to a school attended by her ex-sister-in-law's children, where she tried to detonate a fire-bomb. She was then prevented from entering a day-centre attended by her ex-sister-in-law's daughter while carrying a can of petrol. Next she took the two children to their home, where she gave them milk laced with arsenic. They spat it out because it tasted funny. She then trapped them in the basement with their mother and set the house on fire. They managed to escape.

Dann then went to another school where she pushed a boy into the washroom and shot him dead. During the rampage she shot two other boys and two girls. Next she held the Andrews' family hostage in their home, shooting 20-year-old Philip Andrews in the chest when he tried to escape. She then put the gun in her mouth and killed herself.

found eight children aged from six to 12 had been wounded. He was wounded in the neck as he tried to tend a victim. A SWAT team was then called in.

In a 20-minute spree Spencer had loosed off 30 rounds. She then blithely chatted on the phone to the police. Who was she trying to kill in Cleveland Elementary, Spencer was asked. "No one in particular. I kinda like the red and blue jackets.' She also told a negotiator that it was 'a lot of fun seeing children shot'. And she insisted: 'Nobody likes Mondays.'

Meanwhile, across the road, children were huddling on the floor in abject terror. Spencer barricaded herself in the house and held the police off for nearly seven hours, saying that she was going to come out shooting. However, in the event, the drama of a threatened cowboy-style shootout never materialized, when after the hours-long siege Spencer simply meekly gave herself up. She walked calmly out of the house and put her gun on the ground. Then she turned and went back in. When she re-emerged she handed 150 rounds of .22 ammunition over to the waiting police officers.

'Easy pickings'

'I had no reason for it, and it was just a lot of fun,' she said later. 'The children looked like a herd of cows standing around; it was really easy pickings.' Inside, the police officers found Spencer's father's house cluttered with beer and whiskey bottles, though Spencer did not appear to be intoxicated. The injured were rushed to hospital. Three of them were released after minor treatment, although another five were kept in, two of whom were in a critical condition.

THE REASONS WHY

At first Brenda Spencer refused to explain her actions. She later claimed that for two years after her arrest she had been kept on mind-altering drugs and it was several years before she realized that she had pleaded guilty to first-degree murder.

'People who saw me say I was a zombie during the court hearings,' she said. 'I said what they told me to say. I did what they told me to do.'

However, in 1993 she tried to explain her actions, saying that she had been under the influence of the drug PCP and alcohol at the time of the shooting.

She also claimed that her attorney had conspired to conceal her drug test results. Both her attorney and the state prosecutor vehemently denied this.

At a parole hearing in 2001 she claimed that her violent outburst had been caused by her father who had sexually abused her. 'I have never talked about this before,' she said. 'I had to share my dad's bed till I was 14 years old.'

She claimed that she had not wanted the rifle her father had given her. 'I had asked for a radio and he bought me a gun,' she said. Asked if she knew why he had done that, she said: 'I felt like he wanted me to kill myself.'

She also said she thought she had shot at the school in the hope that the police would kill her at the end of the siege. 'I had failed in every other suicide attempt,' she said. 'I thought if I shot the cops they would shoot me.'

More than 20 years after the shooting, Brenda Spencer became, at long last, penitent. 'I know saying I'm sorry doesn't make it all right,' she said, adding that she now wished it had never happened. 'With every school shooting, I feel I'm partially responsible. What if they got their idea from what I did?' She also claimed not to remember her infamous 'Mondays' comment.

Parole has been denied four times and Brenda Spencer will not be eligible again until 2019.

A bullet passed through the abdomen of eight-year-old Mary Clark, but she did not tell anyone that she had been shot and went back to class. 'She was afraid to talk to anyone,' a policeman said. Several hours later she was taken to hospital where she was found to be in a serious condition.

Bloodstains in the playground

Next day the flag was flying at half mast at Grover Cleveland Elementary School and, when the children arrived, a member of staff was still scrubbing bloodstains from the playground. Understandably some of the children were more than a little wary about returning.

'I had bad dreams and thought the lady would still be here,' said nine-year-old George Johnson as he entered school at around 8.40 a.m. 'But my dad said it's all right now.' Teachers encouraged their students to talk about the tragedy. 'Why did she do it?' asked one bewildered eight-year-old. No one had an answer.

Although she was only 16 at the time, due to the seriousness of the crime, Brenda Spencer was tried as an adult. She pleaded guilty to two counts of murder and assault with a deadly weapon, and was sentenced to a term of 25 years to life in prison.

WOO BUM-KON

South Korea, 26–27 April 1982

Largest spree killing of modern times

Twenty-seven-year-old South Korean police officer

Woo Bum-kon killed 58 people, including himself, and wounded 35 others in a rampage through a mountainous region of Uiryeong county in the province of Gyeongsangnam, South Korea, which lies south of the capital Seoul. His rampage was an eerie harbinger of the killing spree of South Korean student Seung-Hui Cho that would take place at Virginia Tech in 2007, and its repercussions reached right to the top of the Korean administration.

On the day Woo Bum-kon ran amok he had had an argument with his live-in girlfriend, 25-year-old Chun Mai-soon. He left their house that afternoon enraged and went to the police armoury of the Kungyu police station. It was unguarded because officers, who might have challenged him, were at a meeting. Woo began drinking heavily. Once he was sufficiently drunk, he picked up two M2 carbines, 180 rounds of ammunition and seven hand grenades.

He shot his first victim on the street in front of the police station. Then he entered the post office and killed the telephone operators and three other employees, so no one could call for help. After that he ran through a shopping area, indiscriminately firing the carbines and exploding at least two grenades.

Wolf in sheep's clothing

Woo moved from house to house, killing all those people he came across. As a policeman it was all too easy for him to gain entry. People assumed he was there to protect them from the perpetrator, but he shot them. Some were shot in shops; others were killed as they ran into the streets, alarmed by the sound of shooting. Most of the victims were shot, but in one case Woo killed an entire family with a grenade.

'The patrolman came to my house leading a student,' said 52-year-old shopkeeper Shin We-do. 'He asked for a soft drink. I gave him one. He had only one gulp and fired a shot at the student, killing the boy there. Then he fired shots at my wife and two children. They all died on the spot. Running out of the house, I was shot at and hit in the legs.'

Once he had worked his way through one village, Woo Bum-kon moved on to the next, killing as he went. In all, his massacre spread over five villages. Shortly before midnight, the police and military personnel organized a manhunt, but did not catch up with their quarry.

Jumping around like a madman

Survivor Chun Yong-sup, a 45-year-old farmer, said that Woo was 'jumping around like a madman, firing. I was so frightened and could not get to my

> **'Then he fired shots at my wife and two children. They all died on the spot.'**
> Survivor

QIU XINGHUA

Between 18 June and 2 July 2006 47-year-old Qiu Xinghua and his wife He Ranfeng went to the local Tiewadian Temple in northwest China's Shaanxi province on two occasions. Qiu argued with Song Daocheng, a temple manager, who stopped him from moving two objects. According to the prosecutor, Qiu also thought that Xiong Wancheng, the chief of the temple, took liberties with his wife during their stay at the temple, and he became so angry that he made a plan to kill the people there and destroy the temple itself.

On 14 July Qiu returned to the temple in the middle of the night and killed all ten people there with an axe. The victims, nine males and one female aged between 12 and 62, included Song and Xiong. The following night he burned the temple to the ground and escaped.

Two weeks later Qiu injured a farmer named Wei Yikai and his wife Xu Kaixiu and daughter Wei Jinmei in Suizhou, Hubei, a neighbouring province of Shaanxi, near Qiu's home town. Wei died of his injuries. Qiu also stole 1,302 yuan ($163) from Wei, the prosecutor said, though he had no previous criminal convictions nor any indication of mental illness.

Qiu was found guilty and sentenced to death. Some 5,000 yuan ($625) of his personal property was confiscated as compensation for the relatives of the victims. On hearing the verdict, Qiu said he would appeal, adding: 'I am so sorry for the victims and their relatives. I really regret it and hope society will not discriminate against my family.' However, he lost his appeal and was executed by a single shot at 9.57 a.m. on 28 December 2006.

house. I fled into a nearby paddy field until all became quiet near dawn, then returned home.'

In the early hours of 27 April Woo strapped his last two grenades to his body. Entering a farmhouse, he held three people captive at gunpoint, then detonated the grenade, killing himself and his final three victims. Only four rounds of ammunition were left.

When the smoke cleared, the authorities began counting the dead. Initially it was feared that as many as 79 had been killed. The wounded, some of them in a critical condition, had to be transported more than 45 kilometres (28 miles) to the nearest hospital. Appeals for blood donors were broadcast nationwide and emergency supplies were soon rushed to the area.

Inferiority complex

Woo's girlfriend Chun Mai-soon had been seriously wounded but survived. She said later that Woo suffered from an inferiority complex and had been bothered by villagers' comments on the fact that they lived together when they were not married. When word of the massacre reached Seoul, interior minister Suh Chung-hwa rushed to the scene in a police aeroplane. Later the provincial chief of police was suspended from duty. Four other officers were arrested for neglect of duty.

Eventually the recriminations spread all the way up the chain of command and interior minister Suh was forced to resign. He was replaced by former army general Roh Tae-woo, who later became president of South Korea. In a collection for the victims and their families, a total of $700,000 was donated and distributed.

TIMIKA AIRPORT

Also known as Mozes Kilangin Airport, Timika Aiport is in Tembagapura in Papua, Indonesia. At 5 a.m. on 15 April 1996 36-year-old Second Lieutenant Sanurip, a member of the Indonesian Special Forces, began shooting indiscriminately with an automatic weapon at people near an army-run aircraft hanger.

He killed a total of 16 people – three fellow Kopassus special forces officers, eight Indonesian soldiers and five civilians, one of them a pilot for Indonesia's Airfast airline, New Zealander Michael Findlay from Brisbane. Eleven other people were hurt before Sanurip was wounded in the leg and subdued by fellow soldiers.

The shooting coincided with a refuelling stop made by a military transport carrying the bodies of two dead soldiers. Sanurip's unit were in action against the Papuan guerrillas who were holding 11 hostages at the time and he was thought to have been a friend of one of the dead men. However, an official report said that there was no link between the refuelling stop and the shooting and that Sanurip was depressed and ill at the time of the shooting.

'The suspect had a mental problem when he went on this shooting spree,' said the Indonesian Army's Chief of General Affairs, Lieutenant General Soeyono.

Other military spokespersons claimed that Sanurip had been suffering from malaria and that this was the cause of his mental state at the time of the shooting. A court martial concluded that he acted alone. The following year his appeal was quashed and he was sentenced to death.

Such things can happen even in a society as tightly regulated as Red China. On 20 September 1994, 31-year-old First Lieutenant Tian Mingjian, an officer in China's People's Liberation Army, had been reprimanded by his superiors for beating another soldier. He armed himself with a Type 81 assault rifle and began shooting up the military base in the Tongxian suburb of Beijing. He killed five soldiers and officers, including the Communist Party political commissar of the camp, and injured at least ten more before he fled from the army base.

Indiscriminate fire

He then hijacked a jeep and headed for the centre of Beijing, continuing his shooting spree in the Jianguomen district of the city, a bustling transport hub used by thousands of people every day. Tian began to fire indiscriminately at people in the streets. They didn't stand a chance – dozens were killed or wounded before they could run for cover. Soldiers sent after him were ordered to change out of their uniforms, so they would not cause alarm among the public while they were searching for the gunman.

Arriving in Tiananmen Square at 7.20 a.m. Tian jumped out of the jeep. He started shooting people at random and riddled a passing bus with bullets. Seventeen people were killed, among them Iranian diplomat Yousef Mohammadi Pishknari and his son. Dozens were injured along the way as the police desperately tried to apprehend the marauding killer. Eventually Tian was besieged at Yabao Road. Heavy fire from the police forced him to flee into a dead end street. After a 20-minute gun battle he was killed by a sniper.

DENIS LORTIE

Canada, 8 May 1984

Killing the Québécois

Spree killing sometimes takes on a political complexion.
On 8 May 1984 Corporal Denis Lortie stormed Quebec's National
Assembly, whose debating chamber had long been a battlefield
between English-speaking Canadians and the French-speaking
Québécois. Changes were afoot. Just a month previously,
security guards had been replaced by more appealing hostesses
who ushered visitors through the hushed, ornate Renaissance-
style halls. Quebecers had grown increasingly disenchanted
with the ruling Parti Québécois, but none took their grievance
as far as Lortie.

At around 9.45 a.m. Lortie entered the building wearing a beret, green combat fatigues, a flak-jacket and ammunition belts. He sprayed the crowds with sub-machine-gun fire. A party of 50 visiting schoolchildren dived for cover. One of the hostesses was shot and fell to the ground. The gunman ran on up to the second floor where legislative employees were preparing for a committee meeting. There he killed three government employees, wounding 13 others. But it was the politicians who were the target of his attack. However, when he barged into the chamber of the National Assembly, the members were not there. He was too early. The morning session was not scheduled to begin until 10 a.m. 'Where are the MNAs, I want to kill them,' he yelled at staff members. 'I must have made a mistake about the time.'

'That's life'

That was as far as Lortie got in his attempt to destroy the province's ruling Parti Québécois. Nevertheless, standing by the speaker's chair he sprayed the chamber with bullets, sending journalists and staff scuttling for the exits. One of them who was wounded in the arm passed in front of the speaker's chair where the gunman was then sitting. 'I'm sorry for wounding you,' said Lortie, 'but that's life.'

The only person who did not flee from the Assembly chamber was René Jalbert, the 63-year-old sergeant-at-arms. He bravely approached Lortie and offered him a cigarette.

Jalbert discovered that Lortie served in his old army regiment, the 'Van Doos'. The nickname of the Royal 22nd Regiment, 'Van Doos' is a corruption of *vingt-deux*, the French for 22. An infantry regiment, it is the most famous francophone unit in the Canadian Forces. It comprises three regular battalions and two reserve battalions, making it the largest regiment in the Army, with its ceremonial home in La Citadelle in Quebec City.

> **VICTIMS**
> Georges Boyer, 59
> Roger Lefrançois, 57
> Camil Lepage, 54

JEAN CLAUDE NADEAU

One French-speaker was unnerved by Lortie's attack on the National Assembly. Twenty-nine-year-old Quebec City resident Jean Claude Nadeau could not sleep that night. The following day he opened fire with a 20-bore shotgun on a city street in downtown Quebec. A male pedestrian was slightly wounded in the arm, hip and leg, and a female motorist suffered a minor throat injury when a pellet pierced her car window.

Nadeau then took a hostage and barricaded himself in his home, which was quickly surrounded by the police. He surrendered 24 hours later.

Jalbert offered to show Lortie his discharge card, if he would allow it. Lortie agreed. Jalbert persuaded Lortie to show him his own military identification. Jalbert then pulled rank and insisted that Corporal Lortie address him as major. However, Lortie took him hostage. The building was evacuated and, by 11 a.m., the police had it surrounded. Eventually, at 2.25 p.m. they persuaded the gunman to surrender.

'He just wasn't rational,' Jalbert told reporters after his ordeal. 'He just kept talking about how he wanted to impress people.'

Born in Pont Rouge, Quebec, Lortie was a 24-year-old army supply technician with the Royal 22nd Regiment. He was stationed at the Canadian Forces Station Carp near Ottawa, the government's emergency bunker and communications centre in case of nuclear attack, also known as the Diefenbunker after John Diefenbaker who was prime minister of Canada from 1957 to 1963 when the Cold War was at its height. Lortie was responsible for ordering and maintaining army material at the base. He would have had access to weapons, but no authority to take them beyond the perimeter.

Sealed envelope

He had left camp the day before the shooting, claiming that he needed time off to arrange a divorce from his estranged wife. Instead he rented a car and drove to Quebec City. There he took a guided tour of the Quebec Parliament Building. It was a reconnaissance trip. He then rented a room in a motel on Boulevard Laurier for the night. The next day, at 9.30 a.m., Lortie walked into the CJRP radio station in Quebec City and dropped off a sealed envelope containing an audiotape for one of the station's broadcasters, André Arthur. Written on the envelope were the words 'The Life of a Person'. He instructed the radio staff not to open the envelope until 10.30 a.m.

To the staff of CJRP, Lortie looked like a nut. He had a large hunting knife strapped to his leg. When they played the tape, they heard Lortie's critique of the policies of Quebec's Premier René Lévesque and his cabinet, who had been in power since 1976 and were staunch proponents of political independence for Quebec.

Then he began ranting about the government's 1977 legislation. Known in the media as 'Bill 101', the aim of the Quebec Charter for the French Language was to establish French as Quebec's pre-eminent language, at the expense of English. The political tirade grew particularly alarming when Lortie began saying that he planned to decimate

THE PARTI QUÉBÉCOIS

The Parti Québécois was formed in 1968 with the aim of promoting the political, social and economic independence of French-speaking Quebec.

In 1976 it was elected to power and its leader, René Lévesque, became premier of Quebec. In 1977 his government passed 'La charte de la langue française' (Charter of the French Language), making French the official language of Quebec, since 85 per cent of the population of the province spoke French and many did not understand any English.

In 1980 the Parti Québécois held a referendum, seeking a mandate to begin negotiations to establish Quebec's independence from Canada. This was rejected by 60 per cent of the voters. The party was re-elected in 1981, but internal conflict led to the resignation of René Lévesque in 1985. In the 1985 election it was defeated by the Quebec Liberal Party.

the provincial government. 'The government now in power is going to be destroyed,' shouted Lortie. 'It will be a first for Canada.'

Lévesque's ruling Parti Québécois was Lortie's principal target. He said he was going to eliminate its members between 10 and 11 a.m., killing anyone else who got in his way. However, by the time the staff of the radio station had listened to the tape and contacted the police, Lortie's plan was already in action.

Lortie's attack stirred strong emotions across Canada. A few anglophone locals even expressed sympathy for his rampage. Nevertheless most Canadians were horrified. They still believed that spree killing was largely confined to the USA. Lortie's attack on one of their seats of government helped convince them that no one in Canada was safe.

First-degree murder

Of the three killed and 13 wounded, none were politicians. In 1985 Lortie was convicted of first-degree murder, but the court found that the trial judge had made errors while instructing jurors about how they should weigh testimony from psychiatrists heard in the case and ordered a new trial in 1987. This time Lortie pleaded guilty to reduced charges of second-degree murder on three counts. He automatically received a life sentence, but would be eligible for parole after ten years.

Lortie was paroled in 1996, one of the very few spree killers ever to be freed. This was done against the wishes of the victims and their families. Lortie had served just 12 years. However, he has not re-offended. One of the conditions of his parole was

> 'No one will be able to stop me – not the police, not the army – because I am going to carry out destruction and then destroy myself'

that he was not permitted to contact any of his victims or their families. That restriction was lifted in 2007 – though not at Lortie's request – in the hope that it would promote reconciliation. Lortie has since patched up his life and remarried. Chillingly, in 1989 Marc Lepine cited admiration for Lortie as inspiration for his own spree killing.

JAMES HUBERTY

USA, 18 July 1984

The San Ysidro McDonald's massacre

James Oliver Huberty was 41 when he shot 41 people, including himself, in the McDonald's in the San Ysidro area of San Diego, yet his whole life seems to have been a long downhill slide towards the incident. A litany of violence and mental health issues culminated in one horrific California summer's afternoon.

Huberty was born in Canton, Ohio, on 11 October 1942. When he was three he contracted polio. Though he recovered he was left with permanent difficulty walking. In the early 1950s his father bought a farm in the Amish country of Pennsylvania, but his mother, a Baptist, refused to live there and abandoned the family. This had a profound effect on the young James, and he became withdrawn and sullen.

In 1962 Huberty enrolled at a Jesuit community college, graduating with a degree in sociology. But then his career took a morbid turn. He moved on to the Pittsburgh Institute of Mortuary Science, where he obtained an embalming licence. While at Mortuary School he met his future wife, Etna. They married in 1965 and had two daughters – Zelia and Cassandra. The Huberty family settled in Massillon, Ohio, where James worked as an undertaker at the Don Williams Funeral Home. In 1971 there was a blaze at their home in Massillon and the Huberty family was forced to relocate to his hometown of Canton, just a few kilometres away.

Violent family

Following the move, Huberty changed jobs, finding work as a welder for Union Metal Inc. in Canton. A history of violent behaviour surrounded the family. At a birthday party for a neighbour's daughter, Etna instructed her daughter Zelia to physically assault one of her classmates. In a related incident, Etna threatened the child's mother with a 9mm pistol. Although she was arrested, the Canton police failed to confiscate the weapon. James Huberty used it to shoot his German Shepherd in the head when a neighbour complained that the dog was damaging his car.

> **'Society has had its chance. I'm going hunting for humans.'**

There was also violence within the Huberty household. Etna once filed a report with the Canton Department of Children and Family Services that her husband had 'messed up' her jaw. She said that, to pacify Huberty during his bouts of violence, she would produce tarot cards and pretend to read his future. This seemed to calm him, temporarily.

After a motorcycle accident, Huberty was left with an uncontrollable twitch in his right arm. This made it impossible for him to continue as a welder. In January 1984 the Huberty family moved to Tijuana, Mexico. Then they settled in San Ysidro on the US side of the border. They lived in an apartment just three blocks from the McDonald's that would become the site of the massacre. He found work as a security guard in San Ysidro. However, he was dismissed from this position two weeks before the shooting.

VICTIMS

Elsa Herlinda Borboa-Firro, 19
Neva Denise Caine, 22
Michelle Deanne Carncross, 18
María Elena Colmenero-Silva, 19
David Flores Delgado, 11
Gloria López González, 23
Omar Alonso Hernández, 11
Blythe Regan Herrera, 31
Matao Herrera, 11
Paulina Aquino López, 21
Margarita Padilla, 18
Claudia Pérez, 9
Jose Rubén Lozano Pérez, 19
Carlos Reyes, 8 months
Lynn Wright Reyes, 18
Victor Maxmillian Rivera, 25
Arisdelsi Vuelvas Vargas, 31
Hugo Luis Velazquez Vasquez, 45
Laurence Herman 'Gus'
Versluis, 62
Aida Velazquez Victoria, 69
Miguel Victoria-Ulloa, 74

Neighbours said that Huberty may have been using drugs, though his wife denied this. Certainly, his mental health was deteriorating. 'He was not in his right mind,' his wife said. 'He said God was too tall and has a blond beard.'

The day before the massacre, Huberty had called a mental health centre to book an appointment with a doctor. The receptionist misspelled his name as 'Shouberty' and said someone would call him back, but no one did. On the morning of the murders, Huberty took his family to the San Diego Zoo. Then they had breakfast at a McDonald's in the Clairemont district of northern San Diego. After they returned home, it seems Huberty and his wife had a row. He stormed out.

Better target

A witness saw Huberty as he left his apartment and headed down San Ysidro Boulevard carrying at least two firearms. They phoned police, but the dispatcher gave the wrong address to the officers who were sent to intercept him.

Other eyewitnesses said that they had seen Huberty at the Big Bear supermarket. He was seen later at the local post office as well. But it seems that Huberty found the McDonald's to be a much better target. At 3.40 p.m. Huberty walked into the fast-food restaurant wearing camouflage trousers and a black T-shirt. He was carrying a 9mm Uzi semi-automatic – the principal weapon fired in the massacre – a 9mm Browning automatic and a Winchester pump-action 12-gauge shotgun. One of the diners, Mrs Griselda Diaz of Tijuana, who was eating in the restaurant with her younger son, said: 'He came in shooting at everyone. I dived on the floor with my boy and crawled behind the counter.'

Witnesses said that he calmly fired round after round at customers and passers-by. 'I killed thousands in Vietnam,' he said, though there is no record of him ever being in the service, 'and I want to kill more … I am going to kill you all.'

When one weapon was empty, he fired with the others until they were all out of ammunition. Then he casually reloaded and began firing again. In the first ten minutes 20 people died, including four who had tried to run out of the building when

THE COURT CASES

In 1986 Huberty's widow Etna tried unsuccessfully to sue McDonald's and his former employer for $5 million, claiming that the massacre was triggered by monosodium glutamate in McDonald's food and Huberty's work with heavy metals. Indeed high levels of cadmium were found in his body. However, it was not possible to establish where they had come from.

Surviving victims and the families of the dead also tried to sue McDonald's and the local franchisee as the shooting took place on their premises. The suit was dismissed as the company had no duty of care to protect patrons from an unforeseen assault by a murderous madman, nor could they show that the company had not taken every reasonable precaution.

the shooting started. One of them, 11-year-old Omar Hernandez, made it as far as the bike rack before he was shot in the back. Another 11-year-old, David Flores, was also killed. Joshua Coleman fell to the ground wounded. He lay still, singing quietly to himself, and survived.

In panic, Maria Diaz fled with her daughter out of a side door when the shooting started, then realized that she had left her two-year-old son inside. She crept back to the window and saw him sitting obediently in a booth. She motioned him towards the door, nudged it open, and the boy toddled to safety.

The miracle was that anybody escaped at all – ten people came out of the restaurant alive after the massacre. Five had hidden in a storage area. One woman played dead beside her murdered husband. A Mexican couple hid behind chair backs while Huberty made his first killing circuit, then slipped out of the door.

'Take him out'

Huberty fired into the first patrol car that arrived. Officers cordoned off San Ysidro Boulevard and Interstate 5, and quickly issued a Code 10 call for a SWAT team. Outside, three wounded pedestrians managed to crawl the short distance to the post office where a SWAT team had assembled. They had initially been sent to the McDonald's at the border crossing with Tijuana, then were redirected to the McDonald's next to the post office, a short drive away. The delay cost them 15 minutes.

The gunfire was so heavy that the police thought there was more than one gunman inside. The police marksmen held their fire for 77 minutes as it was feared that the gunman might be holding hostages. But they did not attempt to contact Huberty himself by telephone, bullhorn or any other means. 'Our interest in negotiation was gone,' said Police Commander Larry Gore. At 5 p.m. the gunfire slackened. A McDonald's employee crept from the basement where he had been hiding with vital information. Huberty held no hostages. The SWAT team got a green light. 'Fix him in your sights and take him out,' they were told. Officer Chuck Foster took aim with his .308-calibre rifle from the roof of the post office next door. Two other officers fired four rounds, but only Foster's single bullet struck and killed Huberty.

WAYNE LEE CROSSLEY

USA, 24 July 1984

A Rambo-style rampage

Gunman termed 'terroristic'

HOT SPRINGS, Ark. (AP) — A gunman whose murderous rampage at a motel bar began with a traffic ticket and ended with his own death was a 'terroristic person'' who had been banned from taverns all over town, motel workers said yesterday.

Before shooting himself, Wayne Lee Crossley killed four people and wounded two more, authorities said.

The 31-year-old gunman had an arrest record dating back 16 years, including an arrest for assaulting a police officer.

On Tuesday, Crossley and Sgt. Wayne Warwick, 36, wounded each other in a gunfight after Warwick stopped Crossley and three of his companions for a traffic ticket. Then the bleeding Crossley went into The Other Place Lounge and opened fire, killing four people and wounding another.

A special weapons team was dispatched to the motel and arrived while shots were still being fired. Flak-jacketed, carbine-toting officers were posted on the roof, while others searched the three-storey motel room by room for any other suspects.

A man is wheeled to an ambulance after a gunman killed four people at a Hot Springs

his life, that he already knew he was going to die in a shootout.''

The dead were identified as Juanita Allen and Helen Frazee, both of Hot Springs, James Stephens of Little Rock

weapon, said Sgt. Paul Jackson. Warwick was armed with a .357-Magnum.

Crossley's .45-calibre pistol was sent to the state crime lab for examination.

Police said Warwick Cross-

Springs home.

Bleeding from his wound headed to the motel lounge, he had been thrown out before, said motel restaura Linda Schmidt and night a

A 31-year-old unemployed carpenter from Hot Springs, Arkansas, Wayne Lee Crossley fancied himself as a Rambo-style survivalist, and, when drunk, rambled on about 'living wild with nature'. He wore camouflage clothing, was obsessed with guns and had a skull tattoo on his arm. During his regular drinking bouts, he would boast to friends that he was 'going to die in a gun battle with the police'. He was right.

Crossley had regular run-ins with the police. His last rampage began when Sergeant Wayne Warwick stopped his car near Hot Springs' City Hall for a minor traffic violation. Warwick got out of his car and started writing a ticket; Crossley came out shooting. He shot the officer with a .45-calibre pistol, seriously wounding him in the leg and groin. The officer shot back with his .357 Magnum, hitting Crossley and one of three passengers in the car. Crossley, bleeding profusely from a stomach wound, drove the car to the Grand Central Motor Lodge half-a-mile away. He had been thrown out of the motel a few weeks earlier and, on that occasion, threatened the staff as he left, according to waitress Linda Schmidt.

'Die in a gunfight'

The bearded loner – of average height, with greasy blond hair and a slight paunch – had been barred from several other lounges in the area. The manager of the Quality Inn across the road from the murder scene described Crossley as a 'terroristic person'.

'In February, he told one of our clerks, Kelly Meeks, he was going to die in a gunfight,' said Margaret Echols. 'He said he didn't care about his life, that he already knew that he was "going to die in a shootout".'

At the Grand Central Motor Lodge, Crossley walked into The Other Place lounge and shot the bartender with his pistol. Then he grabbed a shotgun from his car and fatally wounded Helen Frazee, the bar's proprietor. He went on to kill two customers, James Stephens from Little Rock and Juanita Allen from Hot Springs, and truck driver Tom Altringer from Fargo, North Dakota, who had stopped to make a phone call. Another visitor was wounded. All of them were unfortunate enough to be in the wrong place at the wrong time.

A SWAT team was despatched to the motel and arrived while shots were still being fired. Officers wearing flak-jackets and carrying carbines were posted on the roof. When the police closed in, they found Crossley's body in the lobby. He had shot himself in the head, though there were also gunshot wounds to his shoulder and chest as well as the earlier wound to his stomach,

> ### VICTIMS
> Juanita Allen, age unknown
> Tom Altringer, 34
> Helen Frazee, age unknown
> James F. Stephens, age unknown
> Sergeant Wayne Warwick, 36

which may have contributed to his death. Officers searched the motel room by room, looking for any other suspects. Crossley's companions in the car were arrested.

Not normal

Crossley had an arrest record that dated back to 1968, including one arrest for assaulting a policeman. He allegedly pistol-whipped his elderly parents, and twice pulled guns on bar-owners who had tried to eject him for rowdiness.

RAMBO

The 1982 movie *First Blood*, starring Sylvester Stallone as John Rambo, brought survivalism to the post-Vietnam war generation. In it Rambo, a misunderstood Vietnam veteran, goes into the woods to take on an overzealous and paranoid local sheriff. As an expert in guerrilla warfare, he outsmarts the sheriff and his men at every turn. The National Guard are brought in. They fire a rocket at Rambo and think they have finished him off. But Rambo escapes and makes a one-man assault on the town and the police station. However, he is dissuaded from killing the sheriff by his Special Forces trainer and – after a diatribe about the horrors of war – turns himself in to the military authorities, who use him on special missions in the subsequent series of Rambo films.

'All I know is Wayne's been awfully depressed the last two weeks,' said Crossley's father, Robert H. Crossley, the day after the shooting. The family home had been put on the market three weeks earlier and was visited by real estate agent Bob Vernon. 'Most of the time I was over there, the boy would just sit around,' he said. 'He just didn't seem normal to me.'

Crossley's drunken fantasies about being alone in the wilderness, self-reliant and living off the land were straight out of the rulebook of the survivalists. This was a movement that sprang up in the 1960s, when people in the United States feared atomic annihilation or imminent invasion by the Soviet Union. Those who thought themselves capable planned to take to the hills and fend for themselves. In the 1970s the threat was seen as the breakdown of society due to social dislocation and racial confrontation, or economic meltdown caused by the collapse of the dollar. This led to a boom in the publication of survivalist tracts. At the end of 1980, *The Alpha Strategy* topped the *New York Times* best-seller list for nine weeks and it remains the bible for survivalists.

In the early 1980s the movement was still strong, supported by books such as survivalist author Ragnar Benson's *Live Off The Land In The City And Country*, published in 1982. With advice on topics such as survival medicine, firearms and preserving food, it proposed that people construct 'survival retreats' to be prepared for the worst, but also to change the way they lived and get back to nature.

With survivalism and the fictional Rambo prominent in the media, was Crossley's spree killing a bloody echo of the times? Over the next decade, the killings of Sherrill, Cruse and Hayes, among others, were to follow Crossley's until, in 1993, action was taken when President Bill Clinton signed the 'Brady Bill' restricting the sales of

THE 'BRADY BILL'

The Brady Handgun Violence Prevention Act was named for James Brady, who was shot by John Hinckley Jr during an assassination attempt on President Ronald Reagan on 30 March 1981. Signed into law by President Bill Clinton on 30 November 1993, it instituted background checks on the purchasers of firearms nationwide in the United States for the first time. Those prohibited from selling, shipping or possessing firearms were any person who:

• Has been convicted in any court of a crime punishable by imprisonment for a term exceeding one year

• Is a fugitive from justice

• Is an unlawful user of or addicted to any controlled substance

• Has been adjudicated as a mental defective or committed to an institution

• Is an alien

• Has been discharged from the Armed Forces under dishonourable conditions

• Having been a citizen of the United States, has renounced US citizenship

• Is subject to a court order that restrains the person from harassing, stalking or threatening an intimate partner or child of such intimate partner

• Has been convicted in any court of a misdemeanour crime of domestic violence.

Any person who is under indictment for a crime punishable by imprisonment for a term exceeding one year was also banned from engaging in interstate or foreign commerce in firearms.

The National Rifle Association vehemently opposed the bill. After it was passed, the NRA funded lawsuits in Arizona, Louisiana, Mississippi, Montana, New Mexico, North Carolina, Texas, Vermont and Wyoming that sought to strike down the Brady Act as unconstitutional.

In its 1997 decision in Printz vs. United States, the Supreme Court ruled that the provision of the Brady Act that compelled state and local law enforcement officials to perform the background checks was unconstitutional as it violated states' rights. However, the overall Brady statute was upheld and state and local law enforcement officials remained free to conduct background checks if they chose. The vast majority continued to do so.

It is estimated that around two million gun sales have been blocked by Brady background checks.

firearms. He related the story of a friend of his who was an Arkansas gun dealer. The gun dealer sold a firearm to an escaped mental patient, who then murdered six people. 'My friend is not over it to this day,' said Bill Clinton as the crowd applauded. 'Don't tell me this bill will not make a difference. That is not true.'

A loophole in the law

Opponents of the bill traced the story back to Crossley's rampage, though only four were killed, not six. And it seems that Crossley did not buy the guns himself but convinced a woman friend to buy them for him. There was nothing in the bill to prevent people with clean records buying guns. Neither was Crossley an escaped mental patient, though he had undergone psychiatric therapy – which again would not disqualify him from owning a gun under Federal law.

Sergeant Wayne Warwick died on 5 September 1986 from a blood clot caused by his earlier injuries. He had been paralysed since the incident.

PATRICK SHERRILL

USA, 20 August 1986

Crazy Pat goes postal

From the mid-1980s to the mid-1990s there was a spate of cases of disgruntled postmen running amok in US post offices, which resulted in the term 'going postal', meaning going on the rampage. The worst case was at Edmond post office in Oklahoma, where Patrick Henry Sherrill killed 14 and wounded six – the third largest mass murder incident of its kind in the United States.

'Fat Pat' or 'Crazy Pat', as he was known by local children, was 16 months into his second stint as a substitute postman. At school he had been an acclaimed sportsman and won a wrestling scholarship to Oklahoma University at the age of 19, but he dropped out in his first year. From his time as a student, he was remembered as odd and a recluse. After a stretch in the Marines, where he was a sharpshooter, he moved back in with his mother in Edmond and enrolled in Edmond Central State University, but again dropped out. He took a series of jobs. At one time he worked for the Post Office, but was sacked because he was rude and uncooperative.

Sherrill lived on the same street in Oklahoma City for 20 years and was notorious in the area for his odd behaviour. He would mow his lawn at midnight, tie up dogs with baling wire or cycle alone on a bicycle made for two. Otherwise he would simply be seen staring blankly out of his window wearing combat fatigues. He was also an avid reader of *Soldier of Fortune*, *Guns and Ammo* and, strangely, *Soviet Life* magazine. He often talked about his time in Vietnam, though in fact he never got further than Camp LeJeune, North Carolina, before he was discharged from the Marines in 1966.

VICTIMS

Patricia Ann Chambers, 41
Judy Stephens Denney, 41
Richard C. Esser Jr, 38
Patricia A. Gabbard, 47
Jonna Gragert Hamilton, 30
Patty Jean Husband, 48
Betty Ann Jarred, 34
William F. Miller, 30
Kenneth W. Morey, 49
Leroy Orrin Phillips, 42
Jerry Ralph Pyle, 51
Paul Michael Rockne, 33
Thomas Wade Shader Jr, 31
Patti Lou Welch, 27

Peeping Tom

Around the neighbourhood he was also known as a peeping Tom. 'Everybody hated him,' said neighbour Gerald Cash. 'He'd prowl around at night, looking in people's windows.' Others disagreed, saying Sherrill was a gentle man who always said 'please' and 'thank you'. The general opinion was that he would not harm a fly.

After his mother died in 1978, most of Sherrill's social contact was via his ham radio set. He remained a reservist though, and in 1984 he joined the Oklahoma National

Guard's marksmanship team. This allowed him to sign out of the armoury his two deadly accurate .45s, as well as a supply of 'woodcutters' – flat-nosed bullets that mushroom out inside their victims. It was these lethal rounds that he used against his co-workers.

With his mother dead, Sherrill needed to work to earn money. He returned to the Post Office as a letter carrier. However, there were complaints about his tardiness and about misdelivered mail. On the afternoon of 19 August 1986 he was publicly reprimanded by two of his supervisors and suspended. Afterwards, he told a female clerk, who had been kind while others had shunned him, not to come to work the following day.

HOMICIDAL TENDENCIES

US Postal Services ordered a national study that showed that USPS employees are no more likely to 'go postal' or commit homicide than other American workers. Between 1992 and 1998 only 16 of 6,719 workplace homicides were attributed to postal employees. According to Jerry Rubenstein, a psychologist at the University of Rochester School of Medicine and Dentistry, the public nature of the job led to postal worker homicides being more highly publicized, thus creating a distorted picture of postal workers' propensity to commit violence.

In fact, the homicide rate in the postal service was considerably lower than in other workplaces, with the retail trade having the highest incidence of occupational homicide. However, a large number of postal employees have embraced this myth, believing that they are at higher risk of dying on the job than others.

Deadly delivery

At 7 a.m. on 20 August Sherrill reported for work as usual. He was wearing his blue US Mail uniform. However, the mailbag slung over his shoulder carried no letters. Instead it contained two .45 Colt semi-automatic pistols, also a .22-calibre pistol and several boxes of ammunition.

Without a word, Sherrill gunned down Richard Esser, one of the supervisors who had upbraided him the day before. The other one, for the first time ever, overslept and turned up to work an hour late, after the shooting had begun.

Sherrill then shot fellow postman Mike Rockne at point-blank range. Next he chased a group of fleeing employees through a side exit, shooting one man who died later in the parking lot. Bolting the doors to prevent anyone escaping, Sherrill pursued his quarry through the labyrinthine corridors of the sorting office. Three were shot at one work station, five at another.

'I froze, I couldn't run'

Debbie Smith was sorting letters when the shooting started. 'I froze, I couldn't run,' she said. 'He came to shoot clerks in the box section next to mine.'

She hid. Sherrill passed her by and opened fire in the next section. As she ran for the door, she said she could hear all the clerks screaming as they were shot. Two employees escaped by hiding in broom cupboards. Another survivor locked herself in a vault where the stamps were kept. When he had emptied his guns, Sherrill stopped

GOING POSTAL

Sherrill was not the only mailman in the USA to 'go postal'.

• Johnstone, South Carolina, 19 August 1983 – former postman Perry Smith killed his former postmaster and wounded two other workers with a 12-gauge shotgun.

• Anninston, Alabama, 2 December 1983 – 53-year-old James Brook shot and killed the postmaster and injured his supervisor with shots to the arm and stomach.

• Atlanta, Georgia, 6 March 1985 – Steven Brownlee, a postman for 12 years, opened fire on the night shift, killing his supervisor and a co-worker, and injuring one other.

• New Orleans, Louisiana, 14 December 1988 – Warren Murphy shot his supervisor in the face with a 12-gauge shotgun, and wounded two other postal employees and two members of a SWAT team.

• Escondido, California, 10 August 1989 – John Merlin Taylor killed his wife, then two colleagues at Orange Glen post office.

• Ridgewood, New Jersey, 10 October 1991 – Joseph Harris shot and killed four people, including his former boss and two other USPS employees, a year after he had been fired.

• Royal Oak, Michigan, 14 November 1991 – Thomas McIlvane killed five people, including himself, with a Ruger 10/22 rifle after he had been fired from the USPS for insubordination and arguing with customers.

• Dearborn, Michigan, 6 May 1993 – Lawrence Jasion, who had worked for the USPS for 24 years, wounded three and killed two, including himself.

• Dana Point, California, 6 May 1993 – Mark Richard Hilburn killed his mother then shot two postal workers dead after being fired from the USPS.

• Goleta, California, 30 January 2006 – Jennifer San Marco, a former postal employee forced to retire for mental health reasons, shot and killed six postal workers before committing suicide. The body of a seventh victim was found at a condominium complex where she used to live. This is thought to be the deadliest workplace massacre by a woman in the USA.

• Baker City, Oregon, 4 April 2006 – Grant Gallaher, a letter carrier for 13 years, ran down and shot dead his supervisor after being assigned a new route.

• San Francisco, California, 28 November 2006 – Julius Kevin Tartt, a postal worker for 18 years, shot his supervisor in the back of the head then shot himself.

and calmly reloaded before beginning again. In 15 minutes he loosed off 50 rounds. One survivor said: 'Imagine your worst nightmare; then scream as loud as you can.'

Among the carnage

The police arrived just minutes after the shooting had started. For 45 minutes they tried to communicate with Sherrill by telephone and bullhorn. There was no reply. A SWAT team went in. They found Sherrill's body among the carnage. After shooting 20 people, he had put a bullet into his own head. His body was found close to that of Richard Esser who had threatened to fire him the day before.

Sherrill's motive was clearly revenge for the public reprimand he had received. However, he had been in practice for vengeance for a long time. In his bedroom the police found ten sets of camouflage fatigues, human silhouettes and dozens of bull's-eye targets nailed to boxes and walls.

CAMPO ELIAS DELGADO MORALES

Colombia, 4 December 1986

The Colombian 'Vietnam veteran'

Several American spree killers claimed to be Vietnam veterans when they had not in fact fought in the war. This may also have been the case with Colombian citizen Campo Elias Delgado Morales, who claimed that he was drafted and saw service in southeast Asia. According to reports, even if Delgado had seen service in Vietnam, he had not been a front-line fighter.

Born on 14 May 1934 in Chinácota, Colombia, Delgado had lived in France, Germany and the United States before he said he was sent to Vietnam as an electrician in 1970. His friend Saul Serrato said that Delgado told him that he had been a crewman on combat aircraft and had fought with US troops. This may be fantasy. But even as a humble electrician he would have been exposed to danger and violence. There were no safe areas in Vietnam. Everyone was in danger from guerrilla attacks. This seems to have had a profound effect on Delgado. When he returned to Colombia, he had changed.

Friends said that his time in southeast Asia had made him antisocial and bitter. 'His experience in the war in Vietnam seems to have been very negative because he hated violence,' said Serrato. While Serrato was convinced his friend was telling the truth, the Pentagon holds no records to indicate that Delgado had served with US military forces in Vietnam.

A terrible lesson

Back in Colombia, Delgado told Serrato that he planned to return to Germany because of the growing guerrilla violence in Colombia and the many street robberies in Bogotá.

Meanwhile, Delgado made a living by giving private English lessons. He also used the money he earned to pay for graduate studies. He was studying French at the Colombian-French institute and attended science classes at the Universidad Javeriana, a Roman Catholic school in Bogotá. However, he was no longer able to develop friendships. Instead of blaming this difficulty with social interaction and relationships on the War, he blamed his mother, Rita Elisa Morales de Delgado, who he lived with in Bogotá. Friends said he beat her. As the years went by, he grew more and more resentful of his mother.

'People are going to know about me real soon. I have a problem. My mother doesn't love me.'

On the afternoon of 4 December Delgado visited the apartment of one of his English students, Claudia Rincón, ostensibly to give her an English lesson. However, during his visit he stabbed 15-year-old Claudia to death, then killed her 34-year-old mother, Nora Becerra de Rincón. Then the dam seems to have burst.

Delgado went back to his own apartment where he killed his mother. He walked up behind her and cut her down with a single stab to the back of the neck. He then loaded his pistol and put it in his briefcase along with five boxes of ammunition. Then he wrapped his mother's corpse in newspaper and clothing and set fire to it. He left his apartment and ran through the building yelling 'Fuego! Fuego!' – 'Fire! Fire!' This brought people out into the hallway. Delgado stabbed one man with a hunting knife.

SATANÁS

In 2002 the acclaimed 'urban realist' novelist Mario Mendoza published the award-winning novel *Satanás* – 'Satan' – based on the Delgado case. Mendoza had met Delgado at the university in Bogotá where Delgado had been a literature student. They had talked just days before the massacre. The book was adapted for the screen by the Colombian film director Andres Baíz and producer Rodrigo Guerrero. Their movie *Satanás* was released in 2007.

Then he opened his briefcase, pulled out his .38 pistol and began firing. At least five people, mostly women, were killed in the apartment complex.

Delgado then visited the home of a former student and her family. Staying for about an hour, he appeared to be calm. Then he headed to an expensive Italian restaurant called Pozzetto in the Chapinero district of Bogotá, discarding his bloodstained hunting knife along the way.

A last meal

Delgado arrived at the restaurant at around 7.30 p.m., found a table and ordered a meal – spaghetti bolognese according to survivors. But in Pozzetto, even this would have been expensive and well beyond the price range of any ordinary Colombian. He washed it down with a copious amount of alcohol – red wine, and eight vodka and tonics.

After about one hour he went to the toilet. When he came out a few minutes later, he walked up to a table where six people were dining. There was a loud exchange of words. Then Delgado pulled out his .38 pistol and shot each of the six people in the head.

Cornered victims

People began screaming and diving under tables for cover. Some crashed through windows while Delgado calmly reloaded. Fortified with food and emboldened with alcohol, he opened fire on other diners. He did this in a chilling, cold-blooded and methodical manner.

Instead of spraying bullets randomly around the restaurant, he walked from one diner to the next, shooting them in the head or neck. He would pick out a specific victim, usually a woman, then go after them. His method was to corner the victim. Ignoring their pleas for mercy, he shot them repeatedly in the forehead at point-blank range. When they were dead, he would move on to the next victim, adopting the same pitiless pattern.

Adults were Delgado's prey and during the rampage he made a promise not to kill any children. However, a six-year-old girl sitting at an adjacent table was killed when his pistol malfunctioned.

FOREIGNERS IN THE VIETNAM WAR

During the Vietnam war, foreign residents in the USA as well as citizens were eligible for the draft. While the Pentagon had no record of Delgado having been drafted into US forces, other countries sent troops. US President Lyndon Johnson initiated a 'More Flags' policy, asking other countries to join the USA in its battle against the communists in Vietnam. Only Australia, New Zealand, South Korea, Thailand, the Philippines and the Republic of China – Taiwan – responded by sending troops.

However, other allies sent material assistance and technicians. Fascist Spain sent a 13-man medical team. The Swiss sent microscopes for Saigon University. Morocco sent 10,000 cans of sardines, while the British sent a printing press for the Saigon government's propaganda department – though they also trained American troops at the British jungle training school in Brunei, and it is rumoured that the SAS went on several covert missions in Vietnam itself.

Delgado was carrying some 400 rounds of ammunition in his briefcase along with an ammunition belt and it was plain that he planned a large-scale massacre. However, while his back was turned, one woman managed to escape. She called the police and they arrived at the restaurant ten minutes later. The horrific carnage that greeted them resembled a scene from a Hollywood gangster movie. By this time, Delgado had shot and killed 21 people, mostly women. A further 15 were wounded, nine seriously.

'He kept shooting and shooting'

'He was a madman,' said fellow diner Juan Guillermo Gomez. 'He kept shooting and shooting … At first we thought the shots were firecrackers. Then we realized it was a madman at the bar, shooting at all of us.'

When the police arrived, Delgado turned his attention to them. A gunfight broke out and he managed to hold them off for about a minute before he died, shot several times in the head. It was claimed that the shots came from police officers. Others say that Delgado himself supplied the fatal bullet, committing suicide before he could be killed or captured.

Expressing his grief over the shootings, Colombia's President Virgilio Barco said that the tragedy should prompt Colombians to reflect on the violence that plagued their country. The government was fighting leftist guerrillas while right-wing death squads had killed around 300 people over the previous year. The country was practically lawless. In 1984 the minister of justice had been assassinated by the drug cartels.

The following year, the M-19 Guerrillas entered the Palace of Justice in Bogotá and took hostages. When the military assaulted the building, around 100 people were killed, including half the Supreme Court justices. Despite the disbandment of paramilitary groups, negotiation with the guerrillas and action against the drug cartels, Colombia remains one of the most violent countries in the world.

WILLIAM CRUSE

USA, 23 April 1987

Librarian turned killer

At 6.30 p.m. on 23 April 1987 61-year-old retired librarian William Cruse rolled up outside the Publix supermarket in the Sabal Palms shopping centre on Palm Bay Road in Palm Bay, Florida, and began shooting. Cruse was a well-known curmudgeon. He shouted at children who took a short-cut across his lawn and, on several occasions, brandished a gun at them. His neighbours had drawn up a petition urging the authorities to do something about Cruse as he was plainly dangerous. They were right.

The first to die in the shootings were two scholarship students from Kuwait – 25-year-old Nabil Al-Hameli and Emad Al-Tawakuly, 18. Also wounded in the barrage were Faisal Mutairi, 19, from Kuwait and Najib Abdul-Samad, 23, from Lebanon. They were studying computer science at the Florida Institute of Technology.

Next Cruse killed Ruth Green and Lester Watson, both locals from Palm Bay. Cruse then began circling the shopping centre in his Toyota, stalking other victims. Bullets skimmed across the façades of storefronts as shoppers dived for cover and doors were slammed and locked. Across Babcock Street, people startled by the sound of gunfire watched fascinated at the commotion, unaware that the source of the shooting was the white Toyota crossing the four-lane highway and heading their way.

Firing from the hip

Sixty-two-year-old jeweller Fletcher Redmond was drawn outside by the sound of gunfire, and found himself confronting the gunman, whose expression was etched on his memory. 'I'll never forget it,' said Redmond. 'It was a wild and desperate look.' He was not far away from the gunman who was firing a semi-automatic rifle from the hip. The gunman was peppering the Winn-Dixie supermarket next door before swinging the weapon in the jeweller's direction.

> ### VICTIMS
> Nabil Abdul Al-Hameli, 25
> Emad Mohamiad Al-Tawakuly, 18
> Ruth Green, age unknown
> Officer Ronald Midgely Grogan, 27
> Officer Gerald Douglas Johnson, 28
> Lester Watson, 51

Redmond ran back inside his store as bullets brought down his front display windows. He ducked behind a showcase. 'I felt one bullet go right through the top of my hair,' said Redmond. 'I just dropped to the floor. I just knew the next shot was going to be lower.'

Jimmie Evans was at a pay phone outside the jewellery store when the gunman aimed at the Winn-Dixie supermarket next door and opened fire. 'I just hit the floor,' Evans said. 'Glass sprayed across everyone.'

The gunman turned to confront a Palm Bay police car that arrived on the scene with its blue lights flashing. Officer Gerald Johnson had been sent to investigate reports of gunfire that had been received five minutes earlier.

Alfred Erbar, who owned the laundromat next door to Redmond's shop, also came out when he heard the gunfire. 'The first police car pulled up about 40 feet away,' said Erbar. 'I looked to my left. There was this man with reddish grey hair, aiming his rifle at the cop behind the wheel before the car stopped. He was just standing there calmly squeezing off shots into the windshield. The cop never had a chance. He just slumped over the wheel.'

Investigators said that eight bullets from a .223-calibre rifle shattered the car windscreen and mortally wounded Officer Johnson – the 28-year-old had only been in the Palm Bay police force for a year. As Officer Johnson lay dying in the front seat of his car, another Palm Bay patrol car arrived. It was driven by 27-year-old Officer Ron Grogan, who had joined the force just seven months before. As Grogan screeched to a halt behind Officer Johnson's vehicle, he came into the sights of the gunman, who was standing partly obscured in the entranceway of the Winn-Dixie store close by. The gunman raised his weapon and took aim.

Picked off like ducks at the fair

The young policeman was mortally wounded before he could step from the car and fell to the pavement, bleeding from at least two wounds. He was crawling on his stomach between the lines of parked cars when Erbar locked the front door of the laundromat and took cover with customers behind the washing machines until Cruse passed. The gunman then entered the Winn-Dixie store, firing at random as scores of shoppers fled. 'It was like we was ducks at the fair or something, male or female or children,' said shopper Marion Ames. She was wounded in the abdomen while her infant son was grazed by a bullet.

Terrified shoppers sprinted out of the back of the supermarket pursued by Cruse. He picked off some of them as they clambered across a wide ditch and fled into the backyards of nearby homes, crying for help and shelter.

Some Winn-Dixie employees took cover inside the store. Three locked themselves in a cold storage room and stayed there until the drama ended nearly eight hours later. Robin Brown, a store clerk, hid in a bathroom. The gunfire ceased. Then she began to panic as she heard footsteps approaching the bathroom door. She saw the handle turn as the door was yanked open.

DEATH SENTENCE

At his trial Cruse pleaded not guilty by reason of temporary insanity. He was convicted of first-degree murder, attempted murder and kidnapping. Although medical experts for both sides agreed that Cruse was mentally ill, the prosecutor argued that, under Floridian law, mental illness is only one factor in a legal definition of criminal insanity. Cruse was given two death sentences, along with four consecutive sentences of life in prison with no possibility of parole for 25 years. He died on death row on 29 November 2009.

DISTURBING INCIDENTS

William Cruse and his wife Millie moved to a redwood-trimmed bungalow in Palm Bay, a growing town some 35 kilometres (22 miles) south of Cape Canaveral, about two years before the shooting. Soon after their arrival, neighbours learnt that Mrs Cruse was seriously ill, though no one could say whether she was suffering from Parkinson's disease or Alzheimer's.

The couple kept to themselves, but there were disturbing incidents. The police were called when Cruse chased some children in his car. He was also reported for making 'lewd remarks' to a boy, but the police did nothing.

As well as trading insults with and bothering the local children, he would also yell at his neighbours in Palm Bay. On one occasion he pointed his rifle at 39-year-old construction worker Ray Carter. 'You made me lose my job,' yelled Cruse. 'I'll get you for this.'

On the evening of the rampage he shot at teenagers in the driveway across the street and at an old blue Chrysler that was parked there. Then he was seen leaving his house with a grey ammunition bag. He got into his Toyota and drove the short distance to the shopping centre.

'I was preparing myself for a bullet,' Brown said. Instead, the gunman told her he needed a hostage. 'I'm sorry I have to do this to you,' he said, putting a revolver against her head.

For the next six hours he kept her and two others hostage as more than 200 policemen and Air Force dog handlers converged on the supermarket. Snipers took up positions on rooftops as medics removed the wounded from the parking lots of the shopping centre. An armoured vehicle was used to remove shoppers who had taken refuge in the parking lot and the area immediately around the shopping centre was cordoned off to keep onlookers away.

Tear gas and stun grenades

A police officer with a bullhorn tried to make contact with Cruse and calm him. 'Bill, we called your wife,' he said. 'She is real disturbed. We are not going to hurt you.' Seeing no way out, Cruse told Robin Brown that he was going to commit suicide. 'I told him to go somewhere else and do it,' Brown said.

Shortly after 2 a.m. he released her and she ran to the safety of police lines. The two other hostages were also released. Police SWAT teams moved in behind tear gas and stun grenades. Cruse threw away his weapons and tried to make a break out of the rear door, but was arrested without a shot being fired. He was charged with six counts of first-degree murder and ten counts of attempted murder. He was not well received at the local jail, where he was greeted by signs posted by inmates saying 'Not insane' and 'Fry his kind'. A second man was arrested in relation to the shootings but was released when it became clear that the carnage was the work of a lone gunman.

After it was all over, five buses rolled out of the shopping centre, crowded with people who leaned out of the windows waving and cheering. They were taken to a nearby store to be interviewed by the police, then to City Hall to be re-united with their relatives.

JOSEF SCHWAB

Australia, June 1987

The Kimberley killer

In the Australian winter of 1987 a cold-blooded double murder sent shockwaves throughout the Northern Territory. The victims were a father and son, Marcus and Lance Bullen, who were shot dead when they were out fishing on the banks of the isolated Victoria River. Initial police investigations failed to uncover any motive for the killings and they were mystified by the crime. It proved to be the beginning of a brief but horrific reign of terror that sparked one of the biggest manhunts in Australian history.

Roadblocks set up on major roads around the area failed to apprehend any plausible suspects. Then a few days later three more tourists – Philip Walkemeyer, Julie Warren and Terry Bolt – were found gunned down in similar circumstances at Pentecost River Crossing between Wynham and Kununurra in Western Australia. It was clear that the killer had eluded the police and escaped across the border from the Northern Territory. The police were now pursuing a gunman engaged in a bloody rampage across thousands of kilometres of wilderness.

Australia on red alert

By now the whole of the 'Top End' of Australia was on red alert. A seven-man team of heavily armed police from the elite anti-terrorist Tactical Response Group in Perth was quickly deployed. But the Kimberley ranges of northern Australia are a wild and inhospitable region where a determined man could hide out for years.

VICTIMS
Terry Bolt
Marcus Bullen
Lance Bullen
Phillip Walkemeyer
Julie Warren

A breakthrough came when keen-eyed outback helicopter pilot Peter Leutenegger from Napier Downs station spotted a camouflaged vehicle in the bush some three hours' drive from Kununurra near Fitzroy Crossing. The police could not be sure if the hidden vehicle belonged to the gunman they were looking for. However, they decided to approach it with caution. They called out a police aircraft to fly over the site in an attempt to flush the occupant out into the open. It worked. An armed man, naked to the waist, emerged from the bushes and began to shoot at police and the aeroplane. As the officers dived for cover in the low-lying scrub, the order was given to open fire. The gunman was shot and wounded but continued to fire at police with his semi-automatic weapon. He clearly had no intention of giving himself up and was finally killed by a gunshot wound to the chest.

The police identified the gunman as a 26-year-old German tourist named Josef Schwab, a security guard in his native country. Later it was found that he had camped on the Bullo River after committing his first murders. Empty cartridge cases were

TIME-LAPSE KILLERS

Josef Schwab's spree was very unusual in that his murderous rampage took place in two separate episodes with several days between them. It was the same with Ronald Gene Simmons. On 23 December 1987, retired Air Force Sergeant Simmons bought a .22-calibre handgun from Walmart and shot his wife, seven children, four grandchildren, son-in-law and daughter-in-law. He also strangled another grandchild with fishing line.

Six years earlier, Simmons had been charged with impregnating his 16-year-old daughter, but the charges were dropped when the family moved from New Mexico to Russell, Arkansas. Simmons ruled his 14-member family with an iron fist. Nothing they did was ever good enough – so he decided to kill them.

Five days after the murders, Simmons drove to Russellville where he shot James Chaffin, a 33-year-old employee of an oil company where Simmons had worked, and 24-year-old Kathy Kendrick, who had rejected his amorous advances. He also shot former co-worker Joyce Butts, and Roberta Woodley. Simmons was sentenced to death for the Chaffin and Kendrick murders, as well as the slaying of his family.

found in the area. Schwab had also carved his name in a boab tree halfway between the Victoria Highway and the Bullo River Station homestead. Lindon Wright, a worker from the station, had seen Schwab with another person in his vehicle, raising the possibility that there might have been another victim. However, locating a body in that vast wilderness would have been next to impossible.

It was later established that Schwab had bought four guns in Queensland, where the gun laws were far less restrictive than in the northern states where the shootings took place. This led to calls for uniform gun laws across the country. Schwab's motive for these apparently random killings remains a mystery, despite over 20 years of investigation. Whatever they were, he took them to his grave.

A lingering legacy

Josef Schwab's deeds of 1987 continue to exert a kind of horrible fascination over the collective consciousness of Australians. In 2006, Foxtel's Crime and Investigation Channel made a documentary about the Kimberley Killer. It contained news footage, interviews with investigators involved in the manhunt and re-enactments of the five murders and final shootout with Tactical Response Group police near Fitzroy Crossing.

Film critics also pointed out that the murders of Phillip Walkemeyer, Julie Warren and Terry Bolt bore an eerie similarity to the fictional movie *Wolf Creek*, released in 2005. The film tells the story of three friends who set off across the rugged Australian outback to see Wolf Creek – a famous crater made by a meteor thousands of years ago at the southern end of Western Australia's Kimberley region. After the three-hour hike to the top of the crater, the three return to their car to find that it will not start. They enlist the help of a seemingly charitable bushman, who happens to be wandering around one of the most remote areas of the world. He offers to tow their car back to his home, where he promises to fix it. However, the three soon discover that he has other plans in store.

ERIC EDGAR COOKE

One of Western Australia's most notorious killers was Eric Edgar Cooke, who went on a murder spree in 1963. On the night of 27 January, Perth poultry dealer Nicholas August was out with barmaid Rowena Reeves. They were sharing a drink in the car around 2 a.m. when Rowena saw a man. Thinking he was a peeping Tom, August told him to 'bugger off'. The man raised a rifle and fired. The bullet nicked August's neck and lodged in Rowena's forearm. Both survived the incident.

Just over an hour later, 54-year-old George Walmsley answered the door bell. He was shot dead on his doorstep. Around the corner, 19-year-old agricultural student John Sturkey was sleeping on the veranda. He was shot between the eyes. Next morning, Brian Weir, who lived nearby in Broome Street, was found with a bullet wound in his forehead. He suffered brain damage and died of his wounds three years later. Three weeks after that the killer struck again. The naked body of 24-year-old social worker Constance Lucy Madrill was found spread-eagled on her back lawn. She had been raped and strangled. The attack had taken place in the woman's own apartment in Thomas Street, while her flatmate, Jennifer Hurse, slept.

On the thundery night of 10 August Carl and Wendy Dowdes returned home to find their babysitter, 18-year-old science student Shirley McLeod, dead. She had been shot with a .22 rifle. Perth was now in a panic. Then on Saturday 17 August an elderly couple were out picking flowers in Mount Pleasant when they found a .22 Winchester in some bushes. The police believed that it had not been discarded but hidden there so it could be used again. They staked out the area for two weeks before a truck driver named Eric Edgar Cooke turned up, looking for the gun.

Cooke had been born in Perth in 1931. Suffering from a hare lip and a cleft palate, he was mocked about his appearance. He was beaten mercilessly by his father. From an early age he suffered severe headaches and

blackouts. These were aggravated by a fall from a bicycle and a dive into shallow water at 14. Doctors suspected brain damage.

Expelled from several schools, Cooke quit education soon after his accident. He took a series of manual jobs, none of which lasted long, before being called up for National Service. In the army he was taught how to handle a rifle.

In November 1953 he married an 18-year-old immigrant from England. Their first child was mentally handicapped and their eldest daughter, one of twins, was born without a right arm. Ostensibly, Cooke was a faithful husband and a loving father, but he began a career of petty thieving. He had burgled some 250 houses and spent three short terms in prison before the police picked him up as a murder suspect.

Cooke confessed to burgling a house in Pearse Street where he found the Winchester. He remembered parking his car again on the way home, then – later – finding the rifle in his hand with a spent cartridge in the breech. He said it was only the next day, when he saw a report about the babysitter's murder on the television, that he realized what he had done.

When the police took him to the scene of Lucy Madrill's murder he confessed to that killing as well. He said he had been robbing the girls' flat when Lucy had woken up. She tried to scream but he throttled her. He strangled her with a lamp flex, then raped her. He dragged her outside, intending to steal a car and hide the body, but when he could not find one he stole a bicycle instead and rode home.

Later he confessed to the murders of 27 January. Cooke also confessed to the murder of 33-year-old divorcee Patricia Vinico Berkman in 1959. She had been stabbed repeatedly in the head and chest. And he said that he had killed the wealthy socialite, 22-year-old Jillian Brewer, later that year, using a hatchet and a pair of scissors. Cooke was hanged in Fremantle Prison on 26 October 1964.

JULIAN KNIGHT

Australia, 9 August 1987

The Hoddle Street massacre

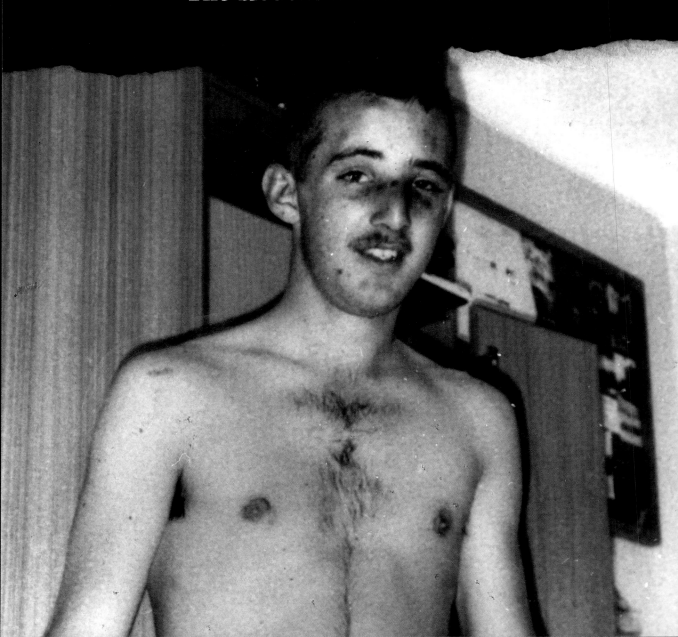

At 9.30 p.m. on Sunday 9 August 1987 Alan Jury was driving along Hoddle Street near the suburb of Clifton Hill, Melbourne, when the windscreen of his car shattered. Realizing that someone was shooting at him, he stamped down on the accelerator. At the next service station he phoned the police and reported that a gunman was firing at passing cars.

In the car behind, Rita Vitcos heard a bang and saw sparks fly off the surface of the road. She too accelerated away. Later, she found two bullet holes in the driver's door. Then 23-year-old Vesna Markonsky's windscreen exploded as she drove down Hoddle Street. She jammed on the brakes. A bullet had hit her in the left arm. As she got out, a second bullet hit her, then a third. Her boyfriend, Zoran Trajceski, who was following in his car, stopped too. So did a young doctor. As the two men ran to tend the dying woman, the doctor fell, hit.

'Kill the bastard'

Another driver pulled up. A bullet hit him in the right temple. He died instantly. A student stopped to help. She too was gunned down. Constable Belinda Bourchier arrived shortly afterwards. Trajceski ran to her and tried to pull her revolver out of its holster. He wanted to 'kill the bastard' who had just murdered his girlfriend, he yelled. More shots screamed past them. They ran for cover behind some trees. More windscreens shattered and cars careered across the road.

A motorcyclist swerved and crashed. As he lay in the road trapped under his bike, two more bullets slammed into his body. One witness reported seeing a victim's body on the road, twitching as the gunman shot it again and again.

After ten minutes of shooting the police turned up in force and established that the shots were coming from the grass verge alongside Clifton Hill railway station. A police helicopter swept the area with a searchlight, but the gunman had vanished.

'A letter of apology constitutes a facet of my rehabilitation and a small measure of making amends for my actions'

A few minutes later a police car, turning into Hoddle Street from the north, came under fire. A policeman at a roadblock there was also winged by a bullet. Another shot struck the helicopter flying overhead, but bounced off its armoured underside.

Close by, two constables managed to trap the gunman in a narrow lane. Out of the darkness came a hail of bullets. One shot hit Constable John Delahunty in the head. He flung himself to the ground and managed to crawl towards the gunman. His partner, Constable Lockman, crawled after him. They got within a few metres of the gunman when the wounded Delahunty saw his head rise above some bushes. Delahunty leapt to his feet and fired his revolver.

LITIGATION

When Knight was not studying, he devoted his time to legal battles with the authorities. In 1992 he appeared before the Administrative Appeals Tribunal challenging the decision not to give him financial assistance to pursue his university studies while in prison. In 2001 he went before the Supreme Court of Victoria asking for papers to be returned that concerned the suicide of a fellow prisoner.

The following year he appeared before the Victorian Civil and Administrative Tribunal asking for papers of a 'political nature' to be returned to him. Their removal, he argued, was a breach of his human rights. The material included two pictures of Adolf Hitler, Nazi insignia, articles concerning the Nazi Party and the Ku Klux Klan, and cards featuring slogans such as 'Stop the Asian invasion', 'We just hate all queers', 'White power' and 'Dial-a-racist' with contact details. He also had pornography, prison rosters, sharpened knives and other prohibited items.

The following month he sought an injunction to prevent the prison authorities inspecting and withholding his legal correspondence. Two weeks later he applied for prison documents under the Freedom of Information Act. A week later he asked for access to the rosters of Barwon Prison under the same Act.

In 2003 he sought a flurry of new injunctions. Ruling that the taxpayer should not have to bear the financial burden of further litigation, a judge ruled that Knight, as plaintiff, should pay costs. Eventually in October 2004, having cost the taxpayer some A$400,000 in legal fees, Knight was declared a 'vexatious litigant' and prohibited from further legal action. He fought that decision too.

The gunman ducked back down behind the bushes. A moment later a voice called out: 'Don't shoot me, don't shoot me.'

Delahunty ordered him to put his gun down and come out with his hands up. A dark silhouette rose from behind the bushes. 'Don't shoot me,' he said again. He identified himself as 19-year-old Julian Knight.

He had recently been discharged from the army after just seven months. Depressed, he had drunk 12 glasses of beer in a local pub. Then he went home to pick up a .22 Ruger rifle, a 7.52mm Norinco M14 military rifle and a 12-gauge pump-action Mossberg shotgun.

He had decided it was time to die, but he said that to commit suicide offended his sense of military honour and he had decided to go down fighting. He had hoped that he might be able to provoke a 'battle' and keep on firing until his ammunition ran out.

Dead or dying

In the space of just 45 minutes Knight had fired at more than 50 cars, hitting 26 people. Seven of his victims were dead, or dying in a nearby hospital. According to Detective Graham Kent, Julian Knight was anything but apologetic. 'He was like a young kid who had been on an adventure and been caught doing something naughty,' said Kent. 'He seemed to be interested in what was happening to him, but not concerned. For a 19-year-old, he seemed very immature.'

Two days later, when what he had done had finally sunk in, Julian Knight had a nervous breakdown and had to be confined to a padded cell. In

THE MAKING OF A KILLER

Knight was an illegitimate child who had been adopted when he was ten days old. His adoptive father was a career army officer, whom he greatly admired, and it was an emotional shock when his parents divorced when Knight was 12.

Although he was generally regarded as bright, his schoolwork soon began to deteriorate. His reports said he was lazy, too easily distracted and too complacent about his abilities. He always had difficulty accepting authority. Unlike other spree killers, Knight was not shy. He had girlfriends and something of a reputation as the class clown at Fitzroy High School. But from an early age he was preoccupied with Charles Whitman and other lone snipers. Eventually he was expelled from school for his violent outbursts.

At school, he had been in the cadet force. He was obsessed with guns and Nazi Germany during the Second World War. At 17 he joined the Army Reserve and served as a trooper in an armoured reconnaissance unit, the 4th/19th Prince of Wales's Light Horse Regiment.

At 18 he was accepted by the Royal Military College at Duntroon, starting there in January 1987. But he performed poorly at his studies and only gained good grades in weapons exercises. An army assessor described him as immature, over-confident and stubborn. He could not knuckle down to army discipline. In May he was charged with eight offences, including four counts of being absent without leave.

Then, on 31 May, after a weekend confined to barracks, he slipped out and got drunk in a nightclub in Canberra. A sergeant found him there and ordered him to leave. Knight stabbed him twice in the face with a penknife. He was charged with assault and discharged from the army in July 1987.

He had no criminal record prior to the Hoddle Street massacre and had a licence for the guns he was carrying.

November 1988 he was sentenced to seven consecutive terms of life imprisonment and told he would have to serve 27 years before he was eligible for parole.

With Knight behind bars, those of his victims who survived still suffer. Steve Wight, who was shot in the back when trying to help other victims, said: 'I have physio twice a week. I still see psychiatrists. As I'm getting older, I'm getting worse. I've had marriage break-ups and haven't worked for 15 years. There's a whole range of issues I still suffer from day to day, night to night.'

Studying behind bars

Meanwhile Knight has spent much of his time behind bars studying. In 1995 he obtained a Bachelor of Arts degree from Deakin University. Although he majored in strategic and defence studies, he also completed sub-majors in international relations, political studies, journalism and psychology. He went on to take additional education courses in information technology, hospitality, engineering, horticulture, cleaning, fitness and first aid.

In 2000, in Barwon Prison, Victoria, Knight found a fellow prisoner who had hanged himself and tried to revive him. His sentence was reduced by three days for meritorious conduct.

MICHAEL RYAN

UK, 19 August 1987

Mayhem in middle England

On 19 August 1987 33-year-old Susan Godfrey took her two children for a picnic in Savernake Forest, not far from the town of Hungerford in Berkshire. At 12.30 p.m., when they had finished eating, she was strapping four-year-old Hannah and two-year-old James into the back of the family car when a man dressed in black appeared. He was carrying an AK-47 and emptied the entire magazine of the Kalashnikov – 15 high-velocity rounds – into her back at point-blank range. The children were later found wandering the forest.

The assailant was 27-year-old Michael Ryan, who lived in the town. On his way home, Ryan stopped at a petrol station, pulled out his rifle and began shooting at the cashier, mother-of-three Kabaub Dean. She dived for cover as the glass window of her booth shattered. Entering the booth, he stood over her with his gun to her head. Ignoring her pleas for mercy, he pulled the trigger. There was a click. He pulled the trigger again and again, but was out of ammunition. Eventually he walked away.

Suburban arsenal

Ryan went home to the house he shared with his mother at 4 South View in Hungerford. There was a steel cabinet bolted to his bedroom wall where he kept a shotgun, two rifles, the 7.62mm Kalashnikov, three handguns and also an M1 carbine and 50 rounds of ammunition which he had bought at the Wiltshire Shooting Centre eight days before the incident. He had joined the club the previous month.

Ryan shot his beloved labrador and his mother. Her body was found lying in the road outside. He set the house on fire and the blaze quickly spread to the three adjoining houses in the terrace. Then he went out again. Neighbour Jack Gibbs flung himself across his wheelchair-bound wife, Myrtle, to protect her as Ryan appeared. Four high-velocity bullets passed through his body, killing him and fatally wounding his wife. She died the next day.

Ryan then shot neighbours Sheila Mason and her 70-year-old father Roland as they fled their home. He gunned down

VICTIMS

Dorothy Ryan, 60, Ryan's mother
Marcus Barnard, 30
PC Roger Brereton, 41
Ken Clements, 51
Jack Gibbs, 66
Myrtle Gibbs, 63
Susan Godfrey, 33
Sandra Hill, 22
Abdul Khan, 84
Roland Mason, 70
Sheila Mason, age unknown
Ian Playle, 34
Eric Vardy, age unknown
Douglas Wainwright, 67
George White, age unknown

MICHAEL RYAN

84-year-old retired shopkeeper Abdul Khan who used to wander the streets from his home in Fairview Road, talking to anyone he met. Ryan also shot at passing cars, killing George White from Newbury who was driving through Hungerford. Ian Playle, who was driving through the town with his wife Elizabeth, his six-year-old son Mark and their 18-month-old baby daughter Elizabeth, was hit several times and died later. Douglas Wainwright was killed in his car on Priory Avenue and his wife was wounded. Eric Vardy was found dead in his car on Priory Road. Cab driver Marcus Barnard was on his way home to his wife and month-old baby when he was shot, while Ken Clements was killed on a footpath at the end of South View.

Ryan's last victim was Sandra Hill. She too was shot in her car on Priory Road. She was rushed to the local doctor's surgery, but it was too late. She died shortly after arrival.

Murderous rampage

In less than an hour and a half Ryan's murderous rampage had left a total of 14 dead and 15 wounded. The police had already been summoned. Shortly after 1 p.m., Police Constable Roger Brereton had arrived in South View to investigate the shooting there. He was calling for back-up when he too was shot. His body was later recovered from his police car not far from Ryan's house. He left a wife and two teenage sons.

The caretaker at John O'Gaunt Secondary School, which Ryan had attended as a child, reported seeing a man enter the school building just before 2 p.m., though it was not until 5 p.m. that the police surrounded it. They made contact with Ryan who seemed lucid and reasonable, though he claimed to be a member of the Parachute Regiment. He admitted shooting his victims but expressed no regret. Only the murder of his mother seemed to bother him. The police held back, fearing that he had taken hostages. At about 6.30 p.m. they heard a muffled shot from inside the school. It was only at 8.10 p.m. that the police burst into the school to find that Ryan had shot himself and was dead.

Hardly a single person in Hungerford's 5,000 population was unaffected. Everyone knew someone who had been killed. While Michael Ryan's mother Dorothy had asked to be buried at Calne in Wiltshire, close to the village of Cherhill where she was born, Ryan himself was to be buried in Hungerford alongside his victims. Some residents of Hungerford muttered darkly that, if he was buried there, his body would be dug up. Instead he was cremated.

GUN LAWS

Prime Minister Margaret Thatcher visited Hungerford two days after Michael Ryan's rampage. She promised to tighten up the gun laws so that such a thing could never happen again. Two years later the Firearms (Amendment) Act was passed, banning semi-automatic and pump-action firearms.

However, in April 1989 22-year-old Robert Sartin committed a 'copycat shooting' similar to Ryan's at Monkseaton, near Newcastle on Tyne, killing one and injuring 14. Then, in 1996, Thomas Hamilton struck in Dunblane, Scotland.

THE MAKING OF A KILLER

Michael Ryan's father Alfred was 55 years old when his son was born. He died two years before Ryan became a notorious spree killer. At the age of 27, Ryan was still living at home with his mother and was thought of as a 'mummy's boy'. Some said that the relationship was 'unhealthy', even that Ryan beat her.

He had been unhappy at school. Other children would try to include him in their games, but he was moody and sulky. Eventually people learnt to leave him to his own devices, though he did suffer some bullying.

From an early age, Ryan developed an interest in guns. At 12 he used to fire a .177 air gun at the cows in the fields behind the house. Later he went out at night to shoot rabbits. One night he had an altercation with a man who was much bigger than him. Ryan pulled a gun and the man fled. 'That just goes to prove the power of the gun,' he said.

Ryan collected ceremonial swords, military badges and medals, and military magazines. Dropping out of school, he drifted through a number of menial jobs. He took out a small-arms licence. Friends said he preferred guns to girls. Gradually he built up his collection. He often boasted to neighbours of the latest gun he had purchased and the sound of him firing in the woods nearby was quite common.

With the death of his father, Ryan became violent and unpredictable. The family were relieved when they heard he was going to marry. A date was set, then the wedding was called off. Some family members thought the whole thing was a sham. They doubted that Ryan ever had a girlfriend at all. He had never been seen with one. His only contact with other people seemed to be through the Wiltshire Shooting Centre in Devizes. It was noted there that Ryan never used targets that showed a human figure, only standard circular accuracy targets.

Although he had no criminal record, Ryan was known to the police. Two months before the massacre, when Ryan had applied to have his firearms licence extended to cover his Kalashnikov, PC Trevor Wainwright, the son of victim Douglas Wainwright, was sent around to Ryan's house to perform a routine check that the gun was stored securely. Finding the cabinet secure, PC Wainwright approved the extension of his licence.

Ryan had been issued a shotgun licence in 1978, when he was just 18. Then on 11 December 1986 he was given a firearms certificate for two pistols. Later he applied to have the certificate amended to cover a third pistol. The story was that he was going to sell one of the two pistols he had, and to buy two more. This was approved on 30 April 1987. On 14 July that year he applied to have the certificate extended once more, this time to cover two semi-automatic rifles, which was approved on 30 July. At the time of the Hungerford massacre, Ryan's considerable arsenal included the following:

• Browning shotgun
• Zabala shotgun
• Beretta 92 semi-automatic 9mm pistol
• CZ ORSO semi-automatic .32 pistol
• Kalashnikov AK-47 7.62mm semi-automatic rifle – Chinese-made Type 56 version
• M1 Carbine .30 7.62mm semi-automatic rifle – a rare version made by the Underwood Typewriter Company.

Ryan used the AK-47 and M1 rifles, and the Beretta pistol in the massacre. The CZ pistol was being repaired at the time. These firearms were all owned legally.

FRANK VITKOVIC

Australia, 8 December 1987

The Queen Street massacre

In 1984 it seemed that Frank Vitkovic was destined for a bright future. He was a good-looking, big-framed youth who was over six feet tall. He had been an excellent high school student, was a star tennis player and now aged 19 he had won a place at Melbourne University's Law School. Even when he dropped out of the course in his final year, no one close to him believed that anything was seriously wrong. The events of December 1987 told a different story.

In mid-September 1987 Vitkovic obtained a gun permit from the Central Firearms Registry in Melbourne after failing just one of 14 questions. It was: 'Should firearms be unloaded before you enter a house or building.' He had answered: 'No.' He then bought an M1 semi-automatic rifle and sawed down the stock and barrel to make the weapon easier to conceal.

On 8 December Vitkovic went to the post office building at 191 Queen Street, Melbourne, where former schoolfriend 22-year-old Con Margellis worked. At 4.10 p.m. he emerged from the lift and greeted Margellis inside the fifth-floor Telecom Employees' Credit Union office. Then Vitkovic brought out his M1 carbine and pointed it at Margellis. It misfired and Margellis dived for cover, then Vitkovic began to shoot indiscriminately. Credit union staff scattered and someone pressed the alarm button. Twenty-two-year-old Judy Morris and her best friend ran towards the glass exit doors, but she was shot dead before she reached them. Meanwhile Margellis took refuge in the women's toilets.

Mayhem hits the post office

The Union office's security doors closed with Vitkovic outside. In frustration, he took the lift up to the 12th floor. The Philatelic Bureau was quiet when Vitkovic burst in, spraying the sales section with rapid rifle fire. The bureau's 29-year-old supervisor, Warren Spencer, was hit as he took cover behind the office photocopier. His wife also worked at the bureau and watched in horror as her husband died. Twenty-year-old Julie McBean and 18-year-old Nancy Avignone were shot dead at their desks.

Crowds gathered on the street below. From a broken 12th-floor window, Vitkovic fired several bullets at the police as they arrived. Running down to the 11th floor, Vitkovic shot 38-year-old Michael McGuire at point-blank range, killing the father of three. In the accounts department, he shot 32-year-old Rodney Brown, who died in the arms of an ambulance man. Thirty-eight-year-old Marianne van Ewyk and Catherine

VICTIMS
Annunziata 'Nancy' Avignone, 18
Rodney Gerard Brown, 32
Catherine Mary Dowling, 28
Julie Faye McBean, 20
Michael Francis McGuire, 38
Judith Anne Morris, 22
Warren David Spencer, 29
Marianne Jacoba Van Ewyk, 38

VITKOVIC'S DIARY

Frank Vitkovic confided to his diary advice for those trying to identify potential spree killers. 'Look for people with a history of rejection, loneliness and ill treatment who also have a fascination with guns and you won't go wrong,' he wrote. Vitkovic had been troubled for some time. Just before his 16th birthday he wrote: 'I know one thing for certain I am hated very much by many people, but they don't know anything of my hatred which is twice as much as theirs … everyone will pay for their sins.'

His motivation was revenge. 'People think I'm worth nothing … I'll treat them as nothing,' he wrote.

The fault, of course, lay with the world. 'The world is full of vicious cruel people,' he had written in 1981. 'There should not be people like that in this world … I will punish these evil vicious cruel scum people.'

These feelings would not go away and by 1987 he was getting ready to do something drastic. 'I'm geared up … I'm a steam train coming through and everyone better get out of the way,' he wrote on 5 December, three days before his rampage.

The following day, things became clearer. 'I can see the paths been laid out for me,' he wrote on 6 December. 'I see those people in the city and I admire them, and yet I hate them 'cos they've been the ones who've lumped shit on me all these years … they have all the things I want but will never have … those greedy businessmen and women in the city … They are all pigs. And pigs always end up in the slaughterhouse.' On 8 December he wrote a note to his parents: 'I've got to get rid of my violent impulses.'

Dowling, 28, were shot dead as they cowered under their desks.

The accounts department assistant manager Tony Gioia then put an end to the massacre. A quiet man who was never known to lose his temper, he tackled the gunman. A head shorter than Vitkovic, he grabbed the killer around the waist. Another of the office workers, Donald McElroy, who had been shot in the shoulder, helped to drag Vitkovic down. Frank Carmody, who had been shot four times, wrested the gun from Vitkovic and Rosemary Spiteri, who had also been wounded, hid it in the fridge.

Vitkovic, who was now bent on taking his own life, struggled to make his way to a window that had been broken in the fracas. Gioia fought to prevent him, grabbing him by the ankles. Office workers in nearby buildings saw the struggle and the shower of glass that preceded the killer as he fell to the pavement a long way below, where he died on impact.

Bodies everywhere

Colin McLaren was the first policeman on the scene. 'There were bodies everywhere,' he said. 'Many people were dead and the rest injured, some were hysterical, screaming or cowering under their desks, or clutching at each other in the corners of the office. None of them could talk.'

The police searched the building in case Vitkovic had an accomplice. At 5 p.m. the Special Operations Group confirmed that the dead man on the street was the lone gunman. They issued an all-clear and an ambulance crew moved in to collect the body. This was the biggest mass killing to have taken place in Australia at the time. It came just four months after Julian Knight's spree, which happened only five kilometres (three miles) away.

THE MAKING OF A KILLER

Vitkovic came from the West Preston area of north Melbourne, home to many European immigrants of the late 1950s and 1960s. His father, Drago Vitkovic, was a house painter from Croatia and the family lived in a small white-painted weatherboard house on May Street. They were the very picture of respectability.

In these affluent surroundings their son Frank thrived. At high school he was placed in the top five per cent of students. He also had a passion for tennis, becoming something of a star on the twin clay courts of St Raphael's tennis club. A strong backhand drive floored many opponents and scared others. This tactic helped him win the club championship in 1983. A former club secretary, Margaret O'Leary, recalled that the sons of other immigrant families in the club – dismissed as 'the ethnics' – idolized Vitkovic. His confidence blossomed. 'The topic of conversation was always Frank Vitkovic,' she said.

Everyone agreed that Vitkovic was destined for bigger things. Nobody was surprised when he won a place at Melbourne University's Law School. To start with everything went fine. Vitkovic told tennis-club friends he was 'breezing through'. But in early 1986 things began to go wrong. Midway through his last year, Vitkovic abandoned his studies and joined his father painting houses.

Vitkovic returned to law school at the beginning of 1987, but it was a brief and unhappy experience. He left his studies again soon after because of 'unsatisfactory progress'. He also sought help from Melbourne University's counselling service during this period. Those who knew him still detected no hint that Vitkovic was having problems. His family were good people and nobody ever expected anything bad to happen to Frank or to be done by him. But after leaving university he stopped working and seemed to lose direction.

Tony Gioia and Frank Carmody were later awarded the Star of Courage, Australia's second highest award for acts of conspicuous courage and bravery.

The deadly effect of life imitating art

As well as his diary, Vitkovic kept a file of newspaper clippings of Julian Knight's massacre on Hoddle Street which he underlined in red, and which the police found after his death. He also had Rambo videos and a number of erotic and violent books in his bedroom. These fed his fantasies. And, like many other spree killers, Vitkovic cultivated a morbid interest in firearms.

His philosophy came direct from the mouth of the fictional John Rambo. 'As Rambo said in *First Blood*, once you accept a problem it's no longer there,' he wrote, and, 'A bullet in the right place seems to do the trick.' Vitkovic also explained his interest in Rambo movies. 'I just like violent films,' he wrote. 'I don't know why. They make me feel better, all the violence gets me pumped up. The sound of the gun going "POW!" It's the only fun I know.' Vitkovic knew he was going to die – in a way he felt dead already. 'Death scares me, but not so much as other people,' he wrote. 'When I go out people don't seem real. I don't feel part of it. I never have really.' The violence of the films may have been one of the few things that punctured his otherwise unreal reality.

MICHAEL HAYES

USA, 17 July 1988

Mad or bad?

On the evening of 17 July 1988 witnesses heard 24-year-old Michael Hayes, the proprietor of Edwards' Moped Sales on Old Salisbury Road, Winston-Salem, North Carolina, walking around his shop firing shots and shouting incoherently. Neighbours had been concerned about his odd behaviour for several weeks and had reported their concerns to the police. 'He would go in and out of his shop, and you could hear him spraying bullets everywhere,' said 49-year-old Nancy Vestal who lived across the road. 'He was yelling like "AGHRRR" and just laughing.'

Volleys of shots were heard coming from the field behind the moped shop off and on between 7 p.m. and 10 p.m. that Sunday. Neighbour 32-year-old Stanley K. Parks, who found Hayes quiet but friendly, said later that he had been acting strangely that night. At about 9 p.m. Parks saw Hayes walking around his shop firing his rifle.

'Before, all he had ever done was shoot into that field down there,' said Parks. 'He kept going in and out, and shooting and yelling.' By 11 p.m. he was worried enough to tell his family to stay in a back bedroom. He also told neighbours O.J. Watkins and Mrs Vestal that they should keep an eye on what Hayes was doing.

A little later, Hayes went out onto Old Salisbury Road, stood on the centreline and began shooting. Stanley Parks was ready for bed when he saw Hayes shooting at a car, apparently without wounding the driver, and called the sheriff. Later Parks discovered that his home had been hit in the rampage.

Adrian Hodges worked at a petrol station near the intersection of Old Salisbury Road and N.C. 150, and at about 11.10 p.m. a man drove in and said he had been shot at. He was in a yellow pickup. There were bullet holes in the passenger side, but the man was not hurt. Hodges called the Sheriff's Department.

Point-blank

Soon after, 21-year-old Melinda Yvonne Hayes was driving south down the road towards her home in Lexington when she was shot. Her car pulled to a stop just past the parking lot of the moped shop. The gunman ran up and fired a second shot at point-blank range, killing her.

Next came 16-year-old Crystal Suzanne Cantrell. She was also travelling southbound down Old Salisbury Road. Hayes fired his .22 rifle at her car. The car then pulled into the parking lot. Eyewitness Tim Beck, who lived with his aunt Mrs Vestal, said that it looked as

VICTIMS
Crystal Suzanne Cantrell, 16
Melinda Yvonne Hayes, 21
Ronald Lee Hull, 32
Thomas Walter Nicholson, 24

though she was trying to turn around and drive away. Whatever her aim, it was to no avail. Hayes fired into the car a second time, killing her too.

Then Hayes shot through the open window of a pickup truck driven by 24-year-old Thomas Walter Nicholson at the intersection of Old Salisbury and Friedberg roads. Nicholson was able to drive around the corner, to the home of a friend and got out of his truck. But he collapsed and died just outside the front door. Pat Fishel was inside.

Her son told her that he had heard shots, but that was not unusual in that neighbourhood. Shortly after, she heard the truck pull into her driveway and the sound of footsteps. She said she looked out of her bedroom window and saw the truck with its door open and the lights on. She did not see Nicholson, who by then was apparently lying on the ground outside her window. Nicholson's body was discovered about 11.45 p.m. by her son-in-law, who had come to make sure that she and her family were all right.

> ## RELEASE
>
> In September 2007 it was revealed that Dix Hospital had allowed Hayes to leave the hospital to work at a petrol station in the Raleigh area. However, the petrol station had had to fire Hayes after receiving anonymous threats that it would be fire-bombed or Hayes would be killed. A number of psychiatrists who cared for Hayes have testified that he should be released from custody. However, in September 2007 Judge Steve Balog denied his release.

Dead on arrival

Thirty-two-year-old Ronald Lee Hull was driving his wife Darlene and eight-year-old son in their Chevrolet when he was hit at the intersection of Old Salisbury and Friedberg. Hayes, Cantrell and Nicholson were all dead on arrival at Forsyth Memorial Hospital. Hull died in the emergency room. Meanwhile 29-year-old Darlene was taken to Baptist Hospital where she was found to be in a 'satisfactory condition'. Their son was uninjured.

Another of Hayes's victims at Baptist Hospital was 28-year-old Jeffery Allen Parks whose condition was 'critical', though he pulled through. Claude E. Eagle Jr, 32, was in a critical condition at Forsyth Memorial. He too survived. Forty-five-year-old James Gray Boyd and Gregory Richard Tirrell, 18, were also treated at Forsyth Memorial for gunshot wounds.

There was initial confusion among the police because the shop lay near the county line between Forsyth and Davidson counties, so no one was sure whose jurisdiction it fell under. Two squad cars arrived. One was hit three times by gunshots and a window was blown out. The other car was hit and Hayes also threatened a rescue-squad worker. Ambulances quickly left the scene and called for back-up. Then at around 11.30 p.m. Hayes was brought down in a hail of bullets fired by sheriff's deputies.

Witnesses said that at least three of the people killed were shot after deputies arrived on the scene, and questions were raised by residents and families of victims about why roadblocks had not been erected to prevent people from driving into the shootings.

THE MAKING OF A KILLER

Michael Hayes was born and brought up in southern Forsyth County, North Carolina. He began to abuse drugs at the age of 13 and became known for his bullying and egotistical behaviour. After leaving school, he bounced from job to job. Eventually his parents bought him his own business, Edwards' Moped Sales, located on Old Salisbury Road in southern Forsyth County. For months Hayes milked funds from the business. In exasperation, his parents threatened to sell the business and stop supporting him. This, it was argued, led to Hayes's final break with reality.

Hayes was taken to Forsyth Memorial Hospital where he was found to be in a critical condition. He survived to be charged with four counts of first-degree murder and eight counts of assault.

At his trial in March 1989 the defence conceded that Hayes had killed four people and wounded five more, but maintained that he was insane at the time. Two psychiatrists and a psychologist testified that Hayes suffered from some form of schizophrenia and was incapable of telling right from wrong at the time of the shootings. Hayes's defence attorney said in closing arguments: 'If you find that Michael Hayes was not insane, you are saying there is no such thing as insanity in North Carolina.'

Cold, cunning and calculating

The District Attorney pointed out that Hayes had purchased the .22-calibre rifle he used just two days before the shootings. 'He said that he wanted a larger calibre gun, he wanted a bigger [ammunition] clip for it,' the DA said. 'He wanted to be, in his own words, a "killing machine". I submit to you that these are the acts of a person who is cold, cunning and calculating and wants to kill people.'

The prosecution also pointed out that Hayes had been a delinquent person all his life – that he had killed pet cats and once hurled a dog out of the window of a speeding car. He used marijuana daily and swore repeatedly during the shootings. 'How many times did he take the Lord's name in vain?' they asked. 'He said, "Roll down the 'goddamn' window you 'motherfucker' at least three times,"' according to the testimony of Darlene Hull. Does that sound like someone on a mission from God?' Mrs Hull testified that Hayes was aiming the rifle at her eight-year-old son when deputies opened fire, wounding Hayes and ending the spree.

During the shooting Hayes called his friend Alan Kemper and said: 'I got a girl. I'm using her as a range marker.' Hayes also called to Kemper to 'get your gun and help me hold off the police'. This proved that Hayes knew he was doing wrong, the prosecution said.

Nevertheless, the jury found Hayes not guilty by reason of insanity and he was sent to a mental hospital. In 1989 Hayes's treatment was discontinued, his psychosis having gone away, but despite his annual petitions to be set free, Hayes remains incarcerated.

CHRISTIAN DORNIER

France, 12 July 1989

Cancelling Bastille Day

On 12 July 1989 31-year-old Christian Dornier killed 14 people and wounded nine others in two small farming villages in eastern France near the Swiss border. It was the bloodiest massacre in France since 1978, when ten people were mown down in a Marseilles bar in what the police said was a gangland killing. And everyone knew it was coming.

'It was a bloodbath,' said Dominique Cuenot of the Luxiol village council. 'He had no friends, hardly ever talked to anybody. We knew he would create havoc one day and the police should have dealt with him a month ago. Unfortunately, our laws don't allow such preventive action.'

The horror began on the afternoon of 12 July when Dornier picked up a double-barrelled shotgun and shot his father, wounding him. He then killed the local vet who had been called out to their farm earlier. After that, he calmly walked up to the family house and blew his mother and his newly-wed sister apart with the shotgun. His sister had been married just six days before.

'There was no argument or quarrel of any kind,' said Dornier's brother later. 'He just picked up his gun and fired it point blank at Corinne, killing her instantly. Then my mother telephoned the police … He fired and killed her too.' Mrs Dornier's phone message raised the alarm and police quickly responded. Forty police officers were involved at the height of the pursuit.

Indiscriminate targets

Dornier walked through Luxiol with a hunting rifle, shooting indiscriminately at anyone who crossed his path. Within three minutes he had killed three young children – one girl who was in the front seat of a car, and a boy and a girl riding their bikes around the village square. An elderly brother and sister also died.

Dornier then walked back home and got into his car. A gendarme tried to stop him but was shot. The mayor's son, Joel Clausse, was upstairs at home when Dornier drove towards the house shooting. He shot at Dornier from an upstairs window with a rifle, wounding him, but not badly enough to stop him. 'I saw blood spurting out of his neck,' said Clausse.

VICTIMS

Corinne Dornier, 26, Christian Dornier's sister

Jeanne Dornier, 57, Christian Dornier's mother

Pierre Boeuf, age unknown

Marie-Alice Champroy, age unknown

Louis Cuenot, 67

Pauline Faivre-Pierret, 5

Louis Girardot, 47

Marcel Lechine, 45

Louis Liard, 50

Marie Périllard, 81

Stanislas Périllard, 79

Georges Pernin, 40

Johann Robez-Masson, 10

Johnny Robez-Masson, 14

CONTINENTAL KILLERS

During the 1980s Continental Europe experienced a spate of spree killings. In April 1983 27-year-old Cevdet Yilmaz shot and killed six people and wounded another five in a café in Delft, the Netherlands. Yilmaz was well educated and a respected journalist, but it was thought he was picked on because of his Turkish origins.

In June that year 34-year-old Karel Charva, a Czech refugee, shot dead five people and wounded 14 others in a school at Eppstein, near Frankfurt. A teacher begged Charva not to shoot the children, but to shoot him instead. Charva obliged, firing seven shots into his face, stomach and left arm. Then he began shooting the children, killing three and wounding 13, four of them critically. He shot another teacher and an unarmed police officer who tried to intervene, before killing himself.

In November 34-year-old Miloud Amrani shot and killed five people, wounding three others, in Lyons. Then in January 1984 Russian teenager Anatoly Markov went on a drunken spree with his father's rifle. He shot at anything he could see – birds, squirrels, the tops of trees. When a helicopter flew over he shot at that too, fatally wounding the flight mechanic. In June 1985 Guy Martell rampaged through a series of towns in Brittany, killing seven and wounding five. In 1987 a Belgian gunman shot and killed seven.

In 1990 three Red Army soldiers went on a shooting spree, killing eight of their comrades, including a lieutenant colonel, at a military depot in the Ukraine. After spraying the depot with machine-gun fire, they escaped in a truck but were captured when it broke down.

Dornier killed four more people before he drove out of the village. His neighbour, Marie-Thérèse Barraud, hid behind a wall as he fired shots into her kitchen. 'My husband, who was outside, was shot in the legs and the head,' she said. She already had reason to fear Dornier. 'I knew he was sick, he had shot at my husband once before. Our neighbours advised us not to go out in our garden.'

A young woman in the village thought the gunshots were firecrackers. 'Then a neighbour told me a black car was driving around the village and the driver was shooting at everybody,' she said. 'I went to tell the mayor. I saw an old woman lying on the ground dead. There were also a lot of injured.'

Arriving in the next village, Autechaux, five minutes away, Dornier killed a farmer on his tractor, along with three passing motorists. He continued through to the next town, Verne, where the police had had time to set up an ambush. There was an exchange of fire. This time Dornier was seriously injured. Once captured by police, he was taken to nearby Besançon hospital for emergency treatment. In Dornier's half-hour spree 23 people had been shot.

Chilling aftermath

With Dornier safely in custody, the inhabitants of Luxiol, which had a population of just 128, took to the streets to inspect the damage and exchange news of friends and neighbours. The car where the young girl was killed was still on the road nearby, its windows smashed and the bodywork riddled with bullet holes. The bicycles belonging to the young girl and boy who had been cycling in the square at the time

ERIC BOREL

Eric Borel was just 16 when he murdered his family in Toulon and went on a killing spree. He was born in 1978 to two serving soldiers, but his parents soon split up and Borel was brought up by his grandparents in Limoges until he was five. Then he went to live with his mother and her new boyfriend, Yves Bichet, who he did not get on with. His mother, who had become religious, beat him.

At first Borel did well at school, but then he began to play truant and started telling tales of his father's heroic deeds during the Indochina War. He had a picture of Adolf Hitler on his bedroom wall and a swastika on his door, and became interested in David Koresh and the Waco siege.

At about 6 p.m. on 23 September 1995 Borel shot his stepfather in the head four times in the kitchen, then beat his head in with a hammer. He killed his 11-year-old half-brother the same way. When his mother came home, he killed her too. Then he set off to the village of Cuers, a short distance away.

He arrived at the home of his only schoolfriend Alan Guillemette at 7.15 the following morning. They spoke in the garden, but when Guillemette turned away Borel shot him in the back, mortally wounding him. Then he began shooting people at random.

He shot Ginette Vialette through an open window. Denise Otto was killed while putting the rubbish out. Her husband Jean was hit in the shoulder. Borel shot an elderly woman in the street, and wounded her husband. Two brothers were also wounded. Rodolphe Incorvala was also shot through an open window. Shopkeeper Mario Pagani was killed while buying a newspaper. Mohammed Maarad was shot in front of the Café de Commerce. Marius Boudon and André Touret were killed while they were drawing money from an ATM and Andrée Coletta while she was taking her poodle for a walk. Finally Borel shot and killed Pascal Moustaki at Place Peyssoneau.

At 8 a.m. the police arrived and Borel shot himself in the head. Two more victims died later in hospital, bringing the death toll to 15. Another four victims survived.

lay near the fountain, while an overturned basket in a garden marked the spot where Dornier had shot a man who had been gathering raspberries.

The celebrations for Bastille Day on 14 July – marking the 200th anniversary of the storming of the Bastille – were cancelled. Flags and bunting were removed from the streets. Instead there was a solemn ceremony with wreaths being placed in memory of the victims. Mourners packed the village's small 17th-century church where eight coffins were lined up.

On 10 November 1989 Dornier was diagnosed with schizophrenia and declared insane. Under French law he could not be held responsible for his crimes and he was never tried for the murders. No one knew what set off the rampage, but his brother claimed that Dornier had never been the same since his military service eight years before. One villager said Dornier was a sour type who never talked to anyone. Townsfolk speculated that the killer had become deranged because of opposition to his sister's recent marriage and his father's refusal to turn over the management of the family farm. Luxiol's mayor, Roger Clausse, whose five-year-old niece was among the dead, said: 'It's appalling, the mountain of sorrow that he has caused.'

JOSEPH WESBECKER

USA, 14 September 1989

The Standard Gravure shooting

When he walked in the main entrance at 8.30 a.m. on 14 September 1989 it had been over a year since Joseph Wesbecker had last worked at Standard Gravure printing works in Louisville, Kentucky. Nicknamed Rocky by colleagues, after the Sylvester Stallone character, Wesbecker was prepared for a lot more than unarmed combat on this occasion. He was carrying a Chinese-made semi-automatic Type 56 assault rifle – a copy of the Russian AK-47 – a SIG Sauer 9mm pistol and a duffel bag containing two MAC-11s, a .38-calibre Smith & Wesson revolver, a bayonet and hundreds of rounds of ammunition.

Born in 1942, Joseph Thomas Wesbecker was just 13 months old when his father, a construction worker, died in a fall. His mother was only 16 at the time and had a hard time coping. His childhood was unsettling. He spent a year in an orphanage. Later he became close to his grandfather, who died when he was four.

Dropping out of school in ninth grade, Wesbecker went to work in the printing industry in 1960, marrying the following year and having two children. When he first went to work at Standard Gravure in 1971 he soon gained a reputation as a hard-working and reliable employee. In 1978 he divorced. There was a bitter battle over custody and child support. It was then that he first sought psychiatric help.

Lonely and isolated

A second marriage lasted only a year. Wesbecker lost touch with much of his family and became lonely and isolated. Work became the centre of his life. However, the company changed hands in 1986 and he became increasingly hostile to the new management, believing that there was a conspiracy to harass him. As a result of his complaint that he was being discriminated against because of his mental condition, he was diagnosed with manic depression and put on Prozac. Meanwhile, he began collecting weapons.

VICTIMS

Richard O. Barger, 54
Kenneth Fentress, 45
William Ganote, 46
James G. Husband, 47
Sharon L. L. Needy, 49
Paul Salle, 59
Lloyd White, 42
James F. Wible Sr, 56

Wesbecker took the lift to the executive suite on the third floor of the printing works. When the doors opened, he loosed off a volley into the reception area, killing receptionist Sharon Needy and putting a bullet into Angela Bowman's back that would leave her paralysed. Looking for his former supervisors, Wesbecker walked through the hallways, calmly shooting anyone he came across. He killed James Husband and injured Forrest Conrad, Paula Warman and John

Stein, a maintenance supervisor, who was shot in the head and abdomen. Then he headed down the stairs to the pressroom, where he killed Paul Salle and wounded two others. Wesbecker's work was precise. There were no bullet holes in the ceiling.

After stashing the duffel bag under a stairwell, Wesbecker walked down to the basement where he meet pressman John Tingle, who was coming to see what all the noise was about. Tingle greeted his former colleague and asked him what was happening. 'Hi John,' replied Wesbecker. 'I told them I'd be back.' Then he warned him: 'Get away from me.'

PROZAC

In August 1989 – less than a month before the shooting – Wesbecker was prescribed Prozac. It did not make him any better. On 11 September he told a psychiatrist that a foreman had forced him to perform oral sex on him in front of his co-workers. The doctor who had prescribed the Prozac advised Wesbecker to come off it. He refused, saying it helped.

After the shooting, the wounded and the families of those killed sued Eli Lilly & Company, the manufacturer of Prozac. The jury found in Eli Lilly's favour, but documents later revealed that the company had already settled with the plaintiffs. According to the medical press, there are some fears that Prozac may provoke suicidal behaviour.

Killed by accident

When Tingle stepped aside, Wesbecker walked on through the basement. He shot Richard Barger in the back, killing him. According to witnesses Wesbecker approached Barger's body and then apologized, saying he had killed him by accident as he could not see who he was shooting at.

Returning to the press floor he shot and killed Lloyd White and James Wible. Then he entered the recreation room where he emptied his magazine, hitting all seven workers present. William Ganote was killed by a shot through the head. After he had reloaded, Wesbecker resumed firing, fatally wounding Kenneth Fentress.

Back in the pressroom Wesbecker took out his SIG Sauer, put it under his chin and shot himself dead. His shooting spree had lasted for around half an hour, leaving eight people dead and 12 wounded. Another of Wesbecker's victims suffered a heart attack during his rampage. In all, he had loosed off approximately 40 rounds of ammunition.

When police searched Wesbecker's house they found more guns – a shotgun, a Colt 9mm, a .32 revolver and a starting pistol. Along with Wesbecker's will, they found a copy of *Time* magazine on the kitchen table featuring an article about Patrick Purdy, who had killed five children and injured 30 others at a school in Stockton, California, earlier that year. Purdy had had a Type 56 assault rifle too.

Wesbecker had been threatening to commit suicide for 20 years, but no one took him seriously. Despite this his medical records showed that he had attempted suicide over 12 times. In 1971 he was well enough to be hired by Standard Gravure. However, he was treated for depression at least three times between 1978 and 1987. According to CBS's *60 Minutes*, in 1984 Wesbecker's medical records showed that he had already

PATRICK PURDY

On 17 January 1989 the police in Stockton, California, received an anonymous threat against Cleveland Elementary School. At midday former Stockton resident Patrick Purdy parked his Chevrolet behind the school and set fire to it. He walked into the playground carrying a Chinese-made Type 56 assault rifle. In three minutes he fired more than 100 rounds, killing five children and wounding 29 others and one teacher. Many of the victims were immigrants from Vietnam and Cambodia – Purdy had regularly complained about Asian immigrants taking Americans' jobs. Purdy then put a pistol to his head and killed himself.

Purdy was found to have a long criminal record and was an alcoholic. He was wearing a flak-jacket with 'PLO', 'Libya' and 'death to the Great Satin' [sic] written on it and had carved the words 'freedom', 'victory', 'Earthman' and 'Hezbollah' into the stock of his assault rifle.

As a result of Purdy's murderous attack, President George Bush Sr banned the import of assault rifles. Wesbecker bought his Type 56 two months after the ban, but it was still legal to own such a weapon provided that it had been imported legally before the ban, and assuming that the owner had the proper permits.

discussed his potential for killing in conversation with his doctor. Have you ever felt like harming someone else, he was asked. 'Yes,' Wesbecker said. Who? 'My foreman.' When? 'At work.'

In May 1987 Wesbecker had filed a complaint with the Jefferson County Human Relations Commission, charging that he had suffered harassment and discrimination due to his psychological state and had been deliberately put under stressful conditions. By 1988 his mental condition was deteriorating and he stopped work that August. His colleague John Tingle said that Wesbecker's doctors had told him the chemical fumes from the plant had made him sick and he was placed on disability leave. Relatives said he was suffering from manic depression, now more commonly known as bipolar disorder. When he bought the assault rifle, Wesbecker had to fill in a form that asked: 'Have you ever been adjudicated mentally defective or have you ever been committed to a mental institution?' He answered no.

Wesbecker had returned to the plant several times over the previous year, but had not threatened his supervisors during these visits. However, he had recently received a letter from the company saying that his disability allowance would be cancelled.

'Kill a bunch of people'

In the years before the shooting, Wesbecker more than once threatened to 'kill a bunch of people' or to bomb Standard Gravure. Before his divorce, he had even told his wife that he was considering hiring an assassin to kill several executives of the company. When he left Standard Gravure in August 1988 he told other workers that he would come back, wipe out the place and get even with the company. It seems he had a grudge against them. One of the company employees said: 'This guy's been talking about this for a year. He's paranoid, and he thought everyone was after him.'

MARC LEPINE

Canada, 6 December 1989

The Montreal massacre

On 6 December 1989, in room 230 on the first floor of the Ecole Polytechnique of the University of Montreal, 60 engineering students were about to finish their last class of the semester. Just before 5.10 p.m. the door flew open. A young man marched into the room carrying a green bin-liner. 'Okay,' he shouted in French. 'Everybody stop what they're doing.' As he spoke, he reached into the bin-liner and pulled out an automatic rifle. The man had a beard, blue jeans, an anorak and a red baseball cap. He looked like a student and everyone suspected this was some kind of end-of-term practical joke.

The man raised the rifle and fired into the ceiling. He divided the class into two – the girls on the left, the boys on the right. Then he told the boys to leave. Still thinking this was some kind of student rag, they filed out. The gunman kicked the door closed behind them.

'Do any of you know why I'm here?' he asked. One of the nine women said no.

'I'm here to fight against feminism,' the gunman said.

'But we are not feminists,' protested 23-year-old Natalie Provost. 'We're just engineering students.'

The moment the words were out of her mouth the gunman started to spray the women with bullets, moving methodically from left to right. Their screams were barely audible above the sounds of automatic fire. Six of the nine fell dead instantly while the other three were badly wounded.

VICTIMS

Geneviève Bergeron, 21
Hélène Colgan, 23
Nathalie Croteau, 23
Barbara Daigneault, 22
Anne-Marie Edward, 21
Maud Haviernick, 29
Barbara Klucznik-Widajewicz, 41
Maryse Laganière, 25
Maryse Leclair, 23
Anne-Marie Lemay, 22
Sonia Pelletier, 28
Michèle Richard, 21
Annie St-Arneault, 23
Annie Turcotte, 20

When he thought he had finished them off, the gunman lowered his rifle and marched out into the corridor. Some of the male students were still there. He fired and they scattered, but he did not seem to want to kill the men: 'I want the women,' he yelled.

Leaning against the corridor wall, he slipped another clip of ammunition into his gun. Then he moved forward down the corridor, continuing to fire at any female students and wounding three more. He also shot and killed a female clerk who was attempting to hide in the finance office.

'He's shooting at everything that moves'

One eyewitness to the carnage was 24-year-old student Daniel Depuis. He had been on the third floor when he heard gunfire. Someone warned: 'Don't go down. He's shooting at everything that moves.' But curiosity drove Depuis to make his way downstairs. He caught a glimpse of the killer who was descending to the foyer.

Depuis went into room 230. One woman was sitting at a desk, bleeding profusely from a gaping shoulder wound and crying hysterically. Depuis made a tourniquet in an attempt to staunch the bleeding. Another woman was lying on the floor nearby. Half her head had been blown away. Outside in the corridor, Depuis discovered two students who were lying together, groaning. Depuis did his best for them, but one died in his arms, the other was dead by the time the ambulance arrived.

The gunman had now arrived in the busy cafeteria on the first floor, where he began shooting again. Three more women were cut down under the Christmas decorations. Other students ran for the exit. The gunman turned and marched back upstairs.

On the third floor, Lepine entered room 311. He fired on the three students who were presenting a project on metallurgy at the front of the class and at the students in the front row, wounding three and killing another. He then shot dead two women as they tried to escape. Some students dived under their desks, while others ran for the door.

The gunman changed the magazine in his rifle and walked towards the front of the class, continuing to fire in all directions. One of the students who had been addressing the class, Maryse Leclair, was moaning and crying for help. A bullet was embedded in her abdomen. The gunman put down his rifle and pulled a hunting knife from his belt. He stabbed her three times, until she gasped and stopped moving.

The gunman then put two boxes of ammunition and his baseball cap on the front desk. He removed his anorak and carefully wrapped it round the end of the rifle barrel. In the eerie silence, some students peered out from beneath their

SUICIDE NOTE

The letter in Marc Lepine's pocket began: 'Forgive the mistakes – I had only fifteen minutes to write this.' He went on to explain his actions.

'Please note that if I am committing suicide today ... it is not for economic reasons ... but for political reasons. For I have decided to send to their forefathers the feminists who have always ruined my life. It has been seven years since that life ceased to bring me any joy, and being totally bored, I have decided to put an end to those viragos ...

'Even if a mad-killer label is stuck on me by the media, I regard myself as a rational and intelligent person who has been forced into taking extreme action ... Being rather backward-looking by nature (except for science), the feminists always have a talent for enraging me. They want to keep the advantages of women ... while grabbing those of the men.'

More rambling anti-feminist rhetoric was followed by a list of 15 local women he wanted dead. 'These nearly died today,' the note ended. 'Lack of time (because I started too late) has allowed these radical feminists to survive.'

THE MAKING OF A KILLER

Marc Lepine was born Gamil Gharbi. His father was Algerian-born businessman Raschid Liass Gharbi. Lepine's mother, Monique Lepine, said her husband thought women were fundamentally inferior to men. Their true role was as servants. She said he was violent, beating her and their children. Gharbi denied this. Marc Lepine's fear of his father continued even after the couple split up after seven years of marriage.

To support her children, his mother worked long hours, leaving Lepine with his older sister Nadine, who treated her shy young brother with open contempt. Though he showed early promise at school, he began to fail academically. He became obsessed with war films and dreamed of joining the army, but was turned down. He also failed to get a place to study engineering at the polytechnic.

At the age of 25 Lepine had his own apartment, but had a running battle with the woman who lived below. He kept a skull on the bookcase. A woman who lived across the street said that she felt he was watching her. He remained extremely shy, had no friends and found it impossible to attract a girlfriend. It seems that he was slowly overtaken by an overwhelming sense of failure and madness. No one ever discovered why he believed feminists had ruined his life.

desks. They saw the gunman put the rifle to his head and pull the trigger. The top of his skull flew across the room. Students rushed to help those who had been hit. The last victim, 23-year-old Maryse Leclair, was dead from a stab to the heart. Three others were also dead. Several other students in room 311 were seriously wounded.

The dead and wounded were already being lifted on to stretchers when the police arrived. A telephone call had alerted them at 5.17 p.m., just three minutes before the gunman ended his life. At 5.26 p.m. Lieutenant Claude Lachapelle of the homicide squad arrived. He ordered that the university security guards were to admit no one else as a precaution against there being another gunman inside. Even the ambulance crews were not allowed to move the wounded until the police were absolutely sure that the killer was dead.

Lachapelle made his way up to classroom 311, where the gunman lay spread-eagled, his brains exposed. The top of his skull, still covered with curly black hair, lay on the other side of the room. The rifle, a .223-calibre Ruger semi-automatic, lay beside him. Lachapelle could not figure out why the killer had gone to the trouble of placing his anorak over the end of the barrel to prevent the blast from burning his flesh when he intended to blow his brains out. A three-page letter, written in longhand in French, was found in his pocket. It was signed 'Marc Lepine'.

> 'Even if a mad-killer label is stuck on me by the media, I regard myself as a rational and intelligent person who has been forced into taking extreme action'

JAMES EDWARD POUGH

USA, 17–18 June 1990

The GMAC massacre

Gunman shoots people hiding under desks

ontinued from Page A-1

e withheld after his probation
eriod, meaning that Pough would
ot have a record in that case if he
eyed the terms of probation. That
ould mean he legally could pos-
ss a gun.

The sheriff said that Pough also
as arrested in 1968 "for dan-
erously displaying a weapon."

McMillan said Pough also has
een positively identified by wit-
esses as the killer of a man and
oman in separate shootings early
nday.

Louis Carl Bacon, 39, and Doretta
rake, 30, were walking through a
orthwest section of Jacksonville,
ear where Pough lived, and were
lled with the same .30-caliber rifle
ed in the Monday massacre,
cMillan said.

McMillan said at least one of the
nday shootings stemmed from
guments over "services of a
ostitute." He did not elaborate.

Records show that Pough was
arried, but neighbors told report-
s they had not seen his wife for
me time.

At the GMAC, five employees, a
stomer and the gunman died at
e scene at the Baymeadows office
mplex, said John Andrews, a
mpany spokesman in Detroit.
wo other employees died at hospi-
s.

The

JAMES EDWARD POUGH
Identified as gunman

taken by ambulance to University
Hospital, Baptist Medical Center and
St. Luke's Hospital, where they
were in critical but stable condition.

Jay Edelberg, of Baptist Medical,
said the three wounded brought
there had been shot repeatedly.

One man had gunshot wounds on
both sides of his chest and in his
abdomen, Edelberg said. A woman
was shot eight times, including both
sides of her chest and her abdomen.

"The third one, who is the most
probably had the worst

injuries because she got hit about
seven times, hitting her arms, her
legs, shattering bones and severing
nerves and arteries," the Baptist
spokesman said.

A special crisis team was at the
shooting scene and police set up a
counseling center in a building next
door.

Investigators were trying to interview witnesses but McMillan said
"the are all in a state of shock,
understandably."

In addition to Pough, the dead

were identified as Drew Woods,
Denise Highfill, Janice David,
Sharon Louise Hall, Barbara
Duckwall Holland, Julia White Bur-
gess, Lee Simonton, and Cynthia
Perry.

The wounded were Ron Ecche-
varia, Jewel Belote, Nancy Dill,
Phyllis Griggs and David Hendrix.

The death total matched the
worst single-day episode in Florida,
a 1982 massacre at a Miami
machine shop where nine died and
three were wounded.

Some tried to run, hide

The Associated Press

JACKSONVILLE, Fla. — Some
employees dashed through a back
door and ducked into neighboring
buildings after a gunman walked
into their auto loan office and
opened fire, killing eight people
before he committed suicide.

"They were running literally for
their lives," said Heather McRae, a
worker at American Transtech,
near the General Motors Acceptance Corp., scene of Monday's
carnage.

Police, GMAC employees and
emergency workers described a
scene of horrible violence inside the
building, with many of the victims
shot as many as eight times.

"It was the worst scene I've seen
we been in the police

department in terms of gruesome-
ness," said Sgt. Steve Weintraub, a
police spokesman with the department for 16 years.

James Edward Pough, 42, entered
the one-story white stone building
about 10:45 a.m. EDT, shot two
customers and then began firing on
employees.

More than 80 employees worked
in the 11,000-square-foot GMAC
office, part of a pine-tree laden
office park that also houses several
AT&T subsidiaries, State Farm Insurance and a variety of small
businesses.

GMAC officials would not allow
reporters into the office, but it was
described as having several rows of
desks laid out in one large room —
offering few obstacles.

*Employees of the GMAC offices in Jacksonville
other after the shootings.*

Cimarron o

When James 'Pop' Pough lived in Jacksonville's Northwest Quadrant, he was known as a quiet man. He worked as an unskilled construction worker and a day labourer. He had been doing maintenance work at a brewery for about a year and his manager considered him one of the company's best workers. He had a good attitude and hardly ever missed work. However, he had a troubled past.

At school in the 1960s he had been involved in gangs. In 1968 he was arrested for the possession of a knife and fined $75. Three years later he was arrested for killing a man outside a bar, but was allowed to plead guilty to aggravated assault and given five years probation. Since, as a result, he had no felony conviction, there was nothing to stop him from buying a handgun.

Pough successfully completed his probation and tried to get his life back on track. However, things began to fall apart when his mother died in 1987. He said he had nothing to live for and would take someone with him when he left this earth. He frequently lost his temper, especially over matters concerning money or his car. His outbursts were often aimed at his wife, Theresa, and he twice put a gun to her head. Fearing for her life, she left him in January 1990 and in March got an injunction preventing him contacting her for a year. He then became withdrawn and rarely socialized. Having his $9,700 1988 Pontiac Grand Am repossessed was almost the last straw. However, worse was to come. After he voluntarily returned the car, the loan company, the General Motors Acceptance Corporation, sent him a bill for another $6,394 – the balance remaining on the loan after they had sold the car.

Two shots to the chest

In the early hours of 17 June 1990 Pough shot a prostitute and a pimp on a corner in Jacksonville not far from her home. Doretta Drake was killed with a single shot to the head from an M1 carbine. Louis Carl Bacon was killed by two shots to the chest. Ten minutes later Pough shot and wounded two youths, aged 17 and 18, after asking them for directions. The police initially assumed that this was a simple prostitution deal gone wrong and only later connected Pough with these killings.

On the morning of 18 June Pough drove to the General Motors Acceptance Corporation offices at 7870 Baymeadows

VICTIMS
Louis Carl Bacon, 39
Jewell Belote, 50
Julia White Burgess, 42
Janice David, 40
Doretta Drake, 30
Sharon Louise Hall, 45
Denise Sapp Highfill, 36
Barbara Duckwall Holland, 45
Cynthia L. Perry, 30
Lee Simonton, 33
Drew Woods, 38

JAMES EDWARD POUGH

Way in Jacksonville. He pulled into the parking lot at around 10.45 a.m. He was well armed. Leaving a 9mm semi-automatic pistol in the boot of his Buick, he walked over to the building and went in through the front door. He was carrying his .38-calibre revolver and an M1 carbine. His pockets were packed with loaded magazines and ammunition. Without a word, he began shooting with the M1 carbine. The first to die was Julia Burgess, a customer standing at the front counter. Pough walked through the open-plan office, moving from desk to desk, systematically shooting at the GMAC workers. He deliberately aimed at people hiding under their tables and those who ducked for cover or tried to escape out of the back.

'Just prayed'

'We realized the guy was pointing his gun underneath people's desks and killing them one by one. I just saw the bottom of the carpet and just prayed,' said one GMAC employee, Richard Langille.

Drew Woods was shot and killed at his desk, followed by Cynthia Perry and Barbara Holland who sat nearby. Forty-two-year-old Phyllis Griggs was also shot and wounded, but survived. Pough shot eight more people, and then put the .38 to his head and killed himself. He had fired 28 rounds from his rifle, hitting a total of 12 of the 85 workers in the office.

'It wasn't random, and it wasn't continuous. It wasn't pandemonium, and at the end we didn't know it was over, because there were silences all through the shooting,' said employee Audrey Hennessey.

Charles Medlin, the building manager at nearby Reichhold Chemicals, saw a woman lying on the grass outside after the shooting and ran over to help. 'She was lying there calm with a stomach wound and a chest wound and just said: "Jesus, don't take me now. I'm not ready to go,"' he said.

THE XEROX MURDERS

Little is known about Bryan Koji Uyesugi except that he had difficulty controlling his temper and left threatening notes for his co-workers. At 8 a.m. on 2 November 1999 he turned up at the Xerox Corporation warehouse in Honolulu, where he had worked as a copier repairman for 15 years, carrying a 9mm handgun and ammunition. Arriving on the second floor he shot two of his colleagues dead. Then he headed for the conference room where he knew a meeting was taking place. There he shot another seven people, five of whom died. Uyesugi was smiling throughout the killing.

He then left the scene and eluded the police for around two hours. He was spotted by a jogger and cornered in the mountains above downtown Honolulu. His brother Denis persuaded him to give himself up. When the police searched Uyesugi's home, they found 17 guns. Some were not registered. He had tried to buy more, but had been denied a permit after being found guilty of destroying property and threatening a supervisor.

Uyesugi was convicted of first-degree murder and sentenced to life imprisonment without parole. He was also ordered to pay $70,000 to the families of his victims. According to the newspapers, he had committed the murders because he feared being fired.

110

CARL ROBERT BROWN

A US Navy veteran, Carl Brown moved from Chicago to Florida, where he became a teacher. Neighbours described him as a quiet, kind and helpful man, though he was plainly disturbed. It was said that he collected tin cans, picked grapefruit from a neighbour's tree in his underwear and would go into other people's yards and yell 'United States' early in the morning. Shots were heard from his house at night and his second wife left him because he would not seek psychiatric help.

Brown's lessons became increasingly incoherent and some children refused to attend. 'He was very prejudiced,' said a fellow teacher. 'He was anti-black, anti-Semitic, anti-everything.'

He was transferred to another school, but his performance did not improve and he was relieved of his duties while he sought psychiatric help. His therapist said that he did not represent a danger to those around him, but refused his request to be allowed to return to work.

On 19 August 1982 Brown fell out with his local repair shop, which had been fixing a lawnmower engine for him, over a bill for $20. The following day he asked his ten-year-old son to join him in 'killing a lot of people', telling him that his final destination would be Hialeah Junior High School.

Brown returned to the repair shop with a 12-gauge Mossberg 500 shotgun and an Ithaca 37 pump-action shotgun with a pistol grip. He walked through the office and workshop, shooting everyone methodically as he went. Reloading several times, he continued until six of the 11 employees lay dead and another two lay dying. The other three, who were wounded, had managed to escape. Then Brown got on his bicycle and rode off.

Mark Kram, an employee of a nearby metal shop, heard of the massacre and picked up a .38 revolver. With Ernest Hammett, he chased after the perpetrator. They caught up with Brown six blocks away. Kram said that he fired a warning shot over Brown's head, but hit him in the back. Brown returned fire, so they ran into him, crushing him against a concrete lamp post. He still had 20 shells in his pocket.

In all, the killing had taken just a few minutes. It was not a frenzied rampage but cold-blooded murder. Some of Pough's victims were shot seven or eight times. Pough died at the scene along with six of his victims. Another three subsequently died in hospital. The last to succumb was 50-year-old Jewell Belote, who died from his wounds nine days later.

The GMAC office never re-opened at Baymeadows Way and the building was subsequently taken over by the Florida Telco Credit Union.

The 'street sweeper'

Once again, in the post-mortem that follows habitually in the wake of a spree killing there were grave political concerns over the weapons the perpetrator was carrying. 'These are military weapons that are very efficient on the battlefield, and if you use them in a GMAC office you are going to get the same effect,' said a Democratic Congressional aide. 'One of the ones sold is called a "street sweeper," and it isn't called that because people use it to shoot moose.'

DAVID GRAY

New Zealand, 13 November 1990

The Aramoana massacre

It was the deadliest criminal shooting in New Zealand's history and it began, like so many other killing sprees, over a trivial matter. At 7.30 p.m. on 13 November 1990 in the seaside town of Aramoana on the North Island of New Zealand, 33-year-old recluse David Gray confronted his neighbour Garry Holden, a 38-year-old automotive electrician, after one of Holden's daughters had wandered on to Gray's property. The matter was unresolved when Gray went into his house, grabbed a Norinco AK-47 assault rifle and shot Holden dead.

Gray then entered Holden's house and shot his daughter, nine-year-old Chiquita, in the arm and chest. Though wounded, she ran outside to raise the alarm and discovered her father's body face down in a pool of blood in the yard. Bleeding heavily, Chiquita ran past the body to the nearby house of her father's partner Julie Ann Bryson. Meanwhile Gray set Holden's house on fire.

Bryson knew that Chiquita's 11-year-old sister Jasmine and her own adopted daughter Rewa, also 11, were also in Holden's house. They had taken refuge under the table when the shooting started. Bryson drove back to Holden's house in her van with Chiquita in an attempt to save the girls' lives. But Gray was standing outside the house, which was now ablaze, and shot at the van.

Gunned down in cold blood

Local men from the town arrived in a utility vehicle to tackle the fire and Gray started shooting at them. Then he gunned down Vanessa Percy as she ran down the street screaming. Her husband, Ross, was driving home from a day's fishing with Leo Wilson, Dion Percy and their sister Stacey in the back of his pickup. The two boys were shot and killed while Stacey suffered severe wounds to her abdomen. Ross Percy was then shot dead, followed by Aleki Tali, who had been fishing with them that day.

Gray then entered the home of Tim Jamieson, killing him and former Green Island mayor Vic Crimp. The next victim was James Dickson, who was out looking for his dog, Patch. Dickson's mother Helen and neighbour Chris Cole went into the road to see what the noise was.

VICTIMS
Rewa Ariki Bryson, 11
Simon Christopher Cole, 62
Victor James Crimp, 71
James Alexander Dickson, 45
Sergeant Stewart Graeme Guthrie, 41
Garry John Holden, 38
Jasmine Amber Holden, 11
Magnus 'Tim' Jamieson, 69
Dion Raymond Jack Percy, 6
Ross James Percy, 42
Vanessa Grace Percy, 26
Aleki Tali, 41
Leo Wilson, 6

Gray shot at both of them, wounding Cole and forcing Mrs Dickson to dive for cover. At 72, she had recently had two hip replacements, was unable to walk without assistance and suffered from restricted arm movement due to surgery.

Cole had been shot in the back and was unable to move. Despite her disabilities Mrs Dickson dragged herself on her stomach some distance to a phone booth to call for help. She then dragged herself back to comfort the man, and crawled home to make further calls. Help arrived too late for Cole, who died in hospital.

Crazed gunman

The first police officer on the scene was Sergeant Stewart Guthrie. Although New Zealand officers do not usually carry guns, Guthrie was an NCO in the Armed Offenders Squad and came armed with a .38 Smith & Wesson police revolver. He enlisted the help of Constable Russell Anderson, who had arrived with the fire service. Arming Anderson with a rifle that he had borrowed from a resident, Guthrie set out to reconnoitre the village. From the extent of the mayhem, it was clear that they were dealing with a crazed gunman. With darkness approaching, Guthrie saw Gray moving about inside his house. He deployed Anderson to cover the front of Gray's home, while he moved to cover the rear. Then a detective and two constables arrived and joined the cordon.

Gray tried to make a break for it out of the front of the property, but Anderson issued a challenge and the gunman quickly retreated. Next he tried to get out of the back. Guthrie, who had taken cover in the sand dunes, spotted him and ordered him to stop. He fired a warning shot and Gray shouted, 'Don't shoot!'

Guthrie thought he was surrendering, but Gray fired several shots, hitting Guthrie in the head and killing him instantly. Units of the Armed Offenders Squad had now sealed off Aramoana. But they kept well back as Gray was armed with a rifle with a telescopic sight, making him dangerous at a distance. Members of the anti-terrorist Special Tactics Group arrived the following morning. They took a reconnaissance flight over the town in an Air Force helicopter, flying high as Gray had already taken pot shots at a news helicopter. Assessing the situation, the STG issued the order 'if he has a firearm, he is to be shot'. After clearing the neighbouring houses, they fired a stun grenade into Gray's home, blowing out the windows, followed by a barrage of tear-gas

THE MAKING OF A KILLER

Born in 1956 in Dunedin on New Zealand's South Island, David Malcolm Gray was quiet and unassuming. 'There was nothing frightening about him then,' said a former classmate. He was, however, a loner. His father died when he was 12 and his mother when he was 29. His sister said this affected him deeply and prompted him to move into the family's holiday home in Aramoana. He worked occasionally as a farmhand, but had been unemployed for several years before the shooting.

Gray was a regular customer at Galaxy Books and Records in Dunedin. The owner, Bill Brosnan, had known him for seven years and said he was an avid reader of military books and *Soldier of Fortune* magazine. Meanwhile he amassed a cache of firearms and ammunition. In January 1990 Gray threatened an assistant of the bookshop with what appeared to be a shotgun in a cardboard box, and Brosnan served him with a trespass notice in February 1990. The police had been warned of his deteriorating mental state.

His sister said he was an animal lover. Residents of Aramoana said this was a source of conflict with his next-door neighbour Garry Holden, whose pets kept dying.

grenades. Judging Gray would by now be out of action, they kicked down the door but found the house was empty. Then they began a house-to-house search down either side of the street. They found Sergeant Guthrie's revolver in a garden, and a woman who had been hiding under a table for more than 20 hours. Meanwhile more units of the Armed Offenders Squad were called in.

After a long day's search, officers came to a small shack at the northeastern corner of the township, screened on both sides with a large hedge. It had a broken window and Gray was spotted inside. The Special Tactics Group tried firing a stun grenade through a window, but it bounced off a mattress that Gray had placed as a barricade and landed back near police. Next they fired tear gas and a gun battle broke out. Gray seemed to be walking around firing at random, and a stray bullet hit an STG officer in the ankle.

'Kill me!'

At around 5.50 p.m. Gray ran out of the house, shooting from the hip and shouting 'Kill me! Fucking kill me!' After several steps, he was knocked down by STG gunfire. Gray was hit five times – in the eye, neck, chest and twice in the groin. Even then he was not dead. He put up a fierce fight with the police officers, at one point breaking free of his plastic handcuffs. He berated the STG officers for not having killed him. An ambulance crew administered oxygen, but he died at 6.10 p.m.

At least 150 police officers were involved in the operation, firing between them 50 to 60 shots. The charred bodies of Jasmine Holden and Rewa Bryson were found in the burnt wreckage of Holden's home. Fourteen people including Gray were dead.

Gray had been carrying a .22 Remington rifle as well as the .223 Norinco when he was shot. Inside the shack police found a .22 Winchester rifle fitted with a silencer, an air rifle, hundreds of rounds of .22 ammunition, and approximately 100 rounds of .223.

GEORGE HENNARD

USA, 16 October 1991

The Luby's Cafeteria massacre

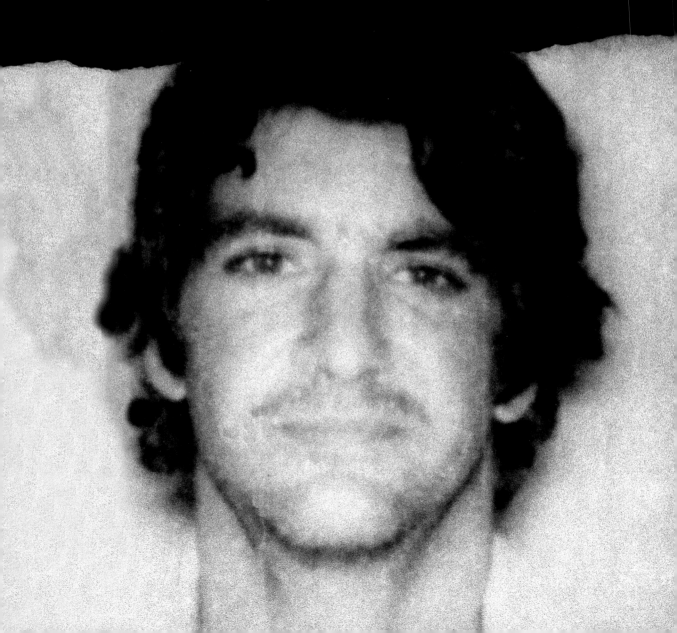

On 16 October 1991 35-year-old George Hennard drove his 1987 Ford Ranger pickup through the plate glass window of Luby's Cafeteria at 1705 East Central Texas Expressway in Killeen, Bell County, Texas, and began a ten-minute orgy of killing that left 23 people dead and 20 injured. It was the deadliest mass shooting in the US until the Virginia Tech massacre in 2007.

It was lunchtime in Killeen and the diner was crowded with around 80 customers. Many of them were taking a break with their superiors on National Boss's Day. 'A lot of people were taking their bosses to lunch,' said 41-year-old Lee Whitney, a Centel manager in Killeen, who was standing with his wife Brenda, 33, at the back of the queue for service when the truck crashed through the window of the restaurant.

'It was really crowded. He immediately started shooting. A lot of shots right away – boom, boom, boom, boom.'

'Texas, this is what you have done for me,' yelled Hennard as he opened fire with two semi-automatic pistols – a Glock 17 and a Ruger P89.

'Today is pay-day'

The first victim was local vet Dr Michael Griffith who had been hit by Hennard's truck as it ploughed through the window. He was trying to get up to help Hennard, when Hennard turned on him.

'Today is pay-day,' said Hennard as he shot him at point-blank range. Then Hennard turned on the lunch queue and started picking off the customers one by one. In his blue T-shirt and dark glasses, Hennard had the blank look of the robot from *The Terminator*, one witness said. It was plain that his intention was to kill everyone.

When his guns were empty, Hennard coolly changed the magazines and continued the slaughter. He reloaded several times during the shooting.

VICTIMS

Patricia Brawn Carney, 57
Jimmie Eugene Caruthers, 48
Kriemhild A. Davis, 62
Lt. Col. Steven Charles Dody, 43
Al Gratia, 71
Ursula Edith Marie Gratia, 67
Debra Ann Gray, 33
Dr Michael Edward Griffith, 48
Venice Ellen Henehan, 70
Clodine Delphia Humphrey, 63
Sylvia Mathilde King, 30
Zona Mae Lynn, 45
Connie Dean Peterson, 55
Ruth Marie Pujol, 36
Su-zann Neal Rashott, 30
John Raymond Romero Jr, 33
Thomas Earl Simmons, 55
Glen Arval Spivey, 44
Nancy Faye Stansbury, 44
Olgica Andonovsk Taylor, 45
James Walter Welsh, 75
Lula Belle Welsh, 64
Iva Juanita Williams, 64

'He had tons of ammo on him,' said Killeen resident Sam Wink. 'He was firing at anyone he could shoot.' Wink said later that the gunman noticed him on the floor and pointed his pistol at him. 'I thought I bought the farm,' he said. But he was saved when a woman got up to run away and Hennard fired at her instead.

HATRED OF WOMEN

The killings may have been motivated by a pathological hatred of women. George Hennard's mother was highly strung and domineering. He had often talked about killing her. According to a friend, he compared her to a snake, picturing her head on top of a rattlesnake's body.

Hennard had written a letter to Jill Fritz and Jana Jernignan – two sisters he was obsessed with – a few months earlier. In it he referred to 'the abundance of evil women' in Killeen and his nearby hometown of Belton. Neighbours said that the police should have done something after Hennard wrote that letter, but the police disputed this. 'There was nothing we could file charges on him for,' Belton Police Chief Roy Kneese said. 'There was nothing in that letter. It seemed like he had a crush on the girls, but there was nothing that in any way discredited them or embarrassed them. It was just a letter.'

A friend, 29-year-old Tim Snyder, said he used to drink in a local park with Hennard, who was called 'Big George'. 'He's nice when he's sober,' Snyder said, 'but when he got drunk he acted berserk. He talked crazy.'

Lee Whitney and his wife also had a narrow escape. Whitney said the gunman 'walked right over my head and there was a lady whose head was eight inches away and he shot her – for some reason, he didn't shoot us.'

Hennard was heard shouting 'You bitch' at one woman before pumping bullets into her defenceless body. However, he showed mercy to another woman. He told Anica McNeil, who was there with her four-year-old daughter Lakeshia, to 'get your baby and get out of here'.

'Tell everybody, Bell County was bad today,' he shouted after them as they scuttled to safety. It was the only time he showed any compassion, but it was to be shortlived. Anica's own mother, Olga Taylor, who was lunching with her daughter and granddaughter, was then coldly gunned down by the deranged killer.

Have-a-go hero

As the massacre continued, 71-year-old retired builder Al Gratia, who had been sheltering behind a table, decided that someone had to do something. He got up and walked towards the crazed gunman. A bullet smashed into his chest. Gratia's daughter, Suzanna Hupp, took the opportunity to escape. She had a gun which she had left in her car. But Gratia's wife, 67-year old Ursula, would not leave her dying husband. As a result she too was killed. Distraught women were hiding under the tables in an attempt to take cover from the gunman. They were screaming and crying, but a number of people managed to escape, thanks to the bravery and quick thinking of hefty car mechanic Tommy Vaughn. He smashed through one of the back windows of the diner and helped 15 people scramble to safety

SUZANNA HUPP

Texas reacted to the massacre, not by tightening up the gun laws, but by liberalizing them.

In 1995 the Texas Legislature passed a 'shall-issue' gun law, which required that all qualifying applicants be issued a Concealed Handgun License – Texas's required permit to carry concealed weapons. This meant that the issuing authority could not deny such licences.

Suzanna Hupp, whose parents Al and Ursula Gratia had been killed at the Luby's massacre while she escaped, campaigned for the law. She had had a handgun in her car which was not far away and regretted that it was not in her handbag. The law at the time prohibited her from carrying the gun with her.

Hupp campaigned across the country in support of concealed-handgun laws. The law in Texas was passed by the then governor, George W. Bush. Hupp herself was elected to the Texas House of Representatives in 1996.

as the gunman bore down on them. One escapee was 67-year-old Killeen resident Betty May, who was having lunch with 60-year-old Evelyn Seales, a friend from the East Side Baptist Church. She said Hennard was almost at her table when Vaughn broke the window behind them. Seizing her chance to fly to safety she leapt up but cut her foot on the glass as she ran through the broken window and needed 14 stitches.

However, it was a small price to pay to safeguard her life. She found Tommy Vaughn afterwards. 'I went up and thanked him,' she said. 'I said, "You saved our lives today. We'd have been dead."'

Hunted like animals

But those who stayed behind in Luby's were tracked down and murdered by Hennard, who showed all the coolness of a professional executioner. Fifty-six-year-old Aden McElveen had found himself trapped under Hennard's jeep as the gunman advanced on him. He was convinced he was going to be next.

'Please give me the satisfaction of some day laughing in the face of all those mostly white treacherous female vipers from those two towns who tried to destroy me and my family'

Then, ten minutes after the shooting had started, Hennard heard sirens wailing outside. The police ordered him to drop his gun. He refused. The police opened fire. In the ensuing gun battle, Hennard was hit twice. He staggered into the back of the restaurant and turned his gun on himself.

Rescuers found a scene of appalling horror. Bodies lay scattered among a battlefield of upturned tables. The wounded were helicoptered out to an army hospital at nearby Fort Hood. 'It was worse than anything I saw in Vietnam,' said one medic.

Twelve hours later one of the restaurant's employees, Mark Mathews, was found alive, hiding in a dishwasher.

WADE FRANKUM

Australia, 17 August 1991

The Strathfield massacre

At around 1 p.m. on Saturday 17 August 1991 33-year-old Wade Frankum went to the Strathfield Plaza, a shopping mall in an upper-middle-class suburb west of Sydney. The two-storey complex of shops, boutiques and small restaurants was filled with customers that afternoon. Frankum took a seat in the Coffee Pot café where he drank several cups of coffee and bided his time.

At approximately 3.30 p.m., apparently without provocation, Frankum pulled a machete from the army surplus duffel bag he had with him and repeatedly slashed one of two teenage girls who were sitting behind him, killing 15-year-old Roberta 'Bo' Armstrong. Leaving the machete sticking out of her body, he pulled an AK-47 out of his duffel bag and, laughing, loosed off shots around the café, killing four more people. Joyce Nixon, 61, and her 37-year-old daughter Patricia Rowe were both cut down by a hail of bullets. Carole Dickinson, her daughter Belinda and her young niece Rachelle Milburn were also hit. Belinda was the only one of the trio to survive.

As the café owner George Mavors walked out of the kitchen, Frankum shot him in the chest. The killer then moved out into the main area of the mall where he killed again, shooting 53-year-old accountant Robertson Kan Hock Joon. Witnesses said the gunman appeared to be calm while screaming shopkeepers and shoppers ducked for cover or fled.

'I grabbed a lady's baby and we jumped over the railings,' said 38-year-old Carolyn Healey, who was in a nearby grocery store when the rampage began. 'We were running, but we could still hear the shooting as if he was coming after us.'

Frankum made his way to the rooftop car park. Belatedly donning a stocking mask, he continued firing indiscriminately from the roof, wounding passers-by below. One person was hit at a railway station close by. Mall workers later found 60 spent shells scattered about the ground.

> ## VICTIMS
> Roberta 'Bo' Armstrong, 15
> Carole Dickinson, age unknown
> Robertson Kan Hock Joon, 53
> George Mavors, age unknown
> Rachelle Milburn, age unknown
> Joyce Nixon, 61
> Patricia Rowe, 37

'Blood was everywhere'

Frankum was still firing as the police arrived at the mall. 'Blood was everywhere,' said Constable George Kohahila. 'People were running frantically around. It was total chaos.'

The gunman then tried to make his escape. He held up a car owner at gunpoint and demanded that she take him to Enfield, a nearby suburb. Before the woman could start her car, the police had blocked the exit. As sirens wailed below, Frankum said: 'I'm

THE PSYCHOLOGY

Criminal psychiatrist Dr Rod Milton presented evidence about Wade Frankum's psychological state before the New South Wales' Coroner and did not think that he was suffering from any mental illness before the shooting. He postulated that four factors motivated Frankum's mass murder: 'Anger, because he was a failure, chronically unassertive and could not tolerate intimacy; guilt, over his mother's suicide; conflict, over his grandmother's estate and certain trivial disputes with the neighbours, and finally; impecuniosity, his money had run out, depriving him of the outlet for his loneliness and sexual needs with prostitutes.' Dr Milton told the court that non-racial mass murder was virtually unknown in Australia until recent years and the gunman was a person of 'essential normality'.

really sorry.' Then he got out of the car, knelt on the ground and shot himself in the head. In just ten minutes Frankum had killed seven people and injured six. He knew none of them.

Frankum had no previous criminal record and there were few clues in his background. His parents were reportedly very strict. They sent him to the exclusive Wesleyan single-sex private school Newington College, where he was bullied for being overweight. He was expelled at the age of 16 for poor attendance. Eventually he got a job at a clothing store and was, by most accounts, a good worker, although not particularly sociable.

Misogynistic violence

Franklin lived alone. In his apartment the police found a large collection of violent videos and literature. Among his books was a copy of the controversial novel *American Psycho* by Bret Easton Ellis. Some have blamed the misogynistic violence in the book for his actions – five of the seven people he killed were women. However, Frankum also owned copies of Dostoevsky's *Crime and Punishment* and Germaine Greer's *The Female Eunuch*.

It was clear that his murderous spree was planned. When he purchased his rifle, he said that he was going to use the firearm to protect himself and, more chillingly, 'wipe people out'.

Frankum had recently inherited A$30,000 after the death of his parents, a legacy which brought him into conflict with the rest of his family. But he squandered the money and could no longer afford the prostitutes that had become an important part of his life. 'Sexual frustration in itself is hardly likely to cause someone to commit mass murder,' psychiatrist Rod Milton told the coroner, 'but in this case sex represented for Frankum the only available area of successful intimacy, even though it was limited and costly.'

It seems likely that Frankum had decided on this course of action in September 1990 when he obtained a gun licence, buying the murder weapon four months later. Around the same time, however, Frankum appeared to try and fight his homicidal tendencies by attending the first of five consultations with a psychologist, which he continued until February 1991. Dr Milton believes seeing a psychologist was Frankum's way of giving the world, as he perceived it, a last chance to redeem itself.

CLIFFORD CECIL BARTHOLOMEW

Although spree killing has traditionally been thought of as an American phenomenon, Australia also has a strong gun culture and a number of Australians have cracked under the strain. In 1971 40-year-old farm labourer Clifford Bartholomew wiped out most of his family. He was living with his wife Heather and their seven children in a dilapidated farmhouse at Hope Forest, near Adelaide, when he lost his job. This put a strain on his marriage.

To make ends meet they took in a lodger, an Australian Vietnam veteran in his twenties. A relationship developed between Heather and the lodger. The Bartholomews spent more time apart, visiting relatives. Sometimes Heather would be accompanied by the lodger. In July 1971 Heather went to visit her sister Winnis in Sydney. While she was away, she wrote a passionate letter to the lodger. Clifford Bartholomew opened it. The lodger left.

When Heather returned home with Winnis and her two-year-old nephew Danny, Bartholomew moved out and went to stay with his stepmother. Sunday 5 September 1971 was father's day and Bartholomew turned up with gifts for his children, who were then aged between four and 19. He had bought his eldest son a .22 rifle. Heather gave him a chilly reception. Harsh words were exchanged. After that he begged his wife for a reconciliation. Heather said she was taking the children to Adelaide where their ex-lodger was arranging accommodation for them.

Bartholomew left. He went back to his stepmother's, but that night he could not sleep. He found it hard to accept that he had lost his wife and family to a younger man. In all the turmoil of the previous day, he had forgotten to give the children their presents. The .22 intended for his eldest child was still in the boot of his car.

Bartholomew devised a plan. He intended to drive over to the house, hit his wife on the head with a rubber-headed mallet, drag her unconscious out to the shed and shoot her – that way he would not wake the rest of the family.

When he arrived at the farmhouse, he loaded the rifle, donned a pair of gloves, crept into his wife's bedroom and hit her on the head – but not hard enough. Heather sat up and screamed. He hit her again, and she fell back on the pillow. 'All of a sudden things seemed dead quiet,' Bartholomew wrote later.

Bartholomew had little recollection of what happened next. It seems that Heather's screams had woken the household – and he killed them. All he could recall was standing in the kitchen with the dead bodies of his wife, his seven children, his sister-in-law and his nephew lying motionless around the house. He phoned his stepmother, who called the police. When they arrived, they found him sitting, drunk, in the kitchen.

'When I got there and walked into the house, I couldn't believe it,' said 17-year-old police cadet Allen Arthur. 'I had never seen so many dead people in one group before and I have not since. You couldn't walk in a straight line through the house down the passageway without stepping over or stepping around dead bodies, it's something I will never forget.'

Bartholomew was tried for only one count of murder. He pleaded guilty to murdering his wife and was sentenced to death. This was later commuted to life. He was a model prisoner and there was an outcry when he was paroled after just eight years.

BARUCH GOLDSTEIN

West Bank, 25 February 1994

Cave of the Patriarchs massacre

According to the book of Genesis, the Cave of the Patriarchs, or the Cave of Machpelah, near Hebron on the Israeli-occupied West Bank, was bought by Abraham from Ephron the Hittite as a burial place for his wife Sarah. It became the family sepulchre. Abraham, his son Isaac and his grandson Jacob, and their wives Sarah, Rebekah and Leah were all buried there. As Abraham is a prophet in the Islamic religion, the caves are a holy place for both Jews and Muslims, who call it the Ibrahimi Mosque.

From the 14th century Jews were forbidden entry to the site and only allowed to come as close as the fifth step on the staircase at the southeast. Later this was increased to the seventh step. After the Six Day War in 1967, the cave came into the possession of the Israelis and the restriction was lifted. The cave was then divided so that both Jews and Muslims could worship there. However, on ten days a year, the cave is reserved solely for Jews and on another ten solely for Muslims.

At 5 a.m. on 25 February 1994, 700 Muslims passed through the east gate of the cave to participate in *Fajr*, the first of the five daily Islamic prayers. It was the holy month of Ramadan and a Friday, the Muslim sabbath. For Jews it was the festival of Purim, which celebrates their deliverance from the Persians in the fifth century BC.

'The harsh reality is: if Israel is to avert facing the kinds of problems found in Northern Ireland today, it must act decisively to remove the Arab minority from within its borders'

Death in a holy place

The cave was being guarded by the Israeli Army, but of the nine soldiers that were supposed to have been on duty, four turned up late and only one officer was present. They did not stop Baruch Goldstein entering the Isaac Hall section of the cave 20 minutes later because they assumed he was entering the tomb to pray in an adjacent chamber reserved for Jews. He was dressed in his reserve captain's olive-green army uniform and a *yarmulke*. He was also carrying an IMI Galil assault rifle and four magazines of ammunition, which held 35 rounds each. This came as no surprise either. As a Jew living in the occupied territories, he was entitled to carry the weapon wherever he went.

He was spotted by mosque guard Mohammad Seiman Abu Sarah, who recognized Goldstein as a well-known troublemaker. Goldstein addressed Abu Sarah in Arabic. 'He asked to go inside during the prayers,' said Abu Sarah. 'I said it is forbidden. He said, "I am the officer in charge here, and I must go in."'

With that, Goldstein knocked Abu Sarah down with the butt of his rifle and rushed into the mosque. Blocking the exit, Goldstein positioned himself to the rear of the

Muslim worshippers, who had just knelt down to pray and were reverently touching their foreheads to the floor.

Goldstein did not say a word. He simply opened fire on the men in rows in front of him. 'I saw seven people die immediately,' said Abu Sarah. 'They were hit in the head, and their brains spilled out. It was total chaos. Everyone was running here and there to try and hide. The mosque was full of blood and wounded people, dead people.'

Swimming in blood

A second guard said: 'People started screaming and running away. Others who were hit were calling for help. People were swimming in blood. It was difficult to distinguish between the dead and the living, because everyone was covered in blood.'

Worshippers raced outside with bodies and jammed them into ambulances without pausing to sort the living from the dead. Ambulance driver Khaled Jaabry discovered only when he reached a local hospital that among the wounded he carried there were his own son and brother.

The firing continued for about ten minutes. It was alleged that some worshippers were shot by Israeli soldiers amid the chaos that Goldstein started. The second guard said he saw three men in Israeli army uniforms enter the mosque and shoot. Israeli TV, quoting army sources, said that two soldiers rushed into the mosque, saw worshippers starting to overpower Goldstein and believed that Palestinians were attacking a uniformed Israeli, so opened fire. The Palestine Liberation Organization also claimed that eight worshippers were killed at the mosque entrance by Israeli soldiers. The Israeli Army did concede that when the worshippers began pouring out of the mosque, soldiers opened fire, but only with warning shots in the air. Military

YITZHAK RABIN

Israeli Prime Minister Yitzhak Rabin condemned Goldstein as 'a villainous Jew' and 'a Jewish Hamas member'. He told the Palestinians that murderous settlers were to be treated as outcasts, alien to Israel and to Judaism.

'I am shamed over the disgrace imposed upon us by a degenerate murderer,' he said. Addressing the most militant settlers, Rabin continued: 'You are not part of the community of Israel. You are not part of the national democratic camp which we all belong to in this house, and many of the people despise you. You are not partners in the Zionist enterprise. You are a foreign implant. You are an errant weed. Sensible Judaism spits you out. You placed yourself outside the wall of Jewish law. You are a shame on Zionism and an embarrassment to Judaism.'

Eli Goldschmidt, a member of the Labour Party, urged Rabin to go further to amend the Law of Return, under which all Jews have the right to immigrate to Israel, and prevent the followers of Rabbi Kahane entering the country. At that time, only Jews who had committed acts against the Jewish people or were a danger to public health or national security or had a criminal record could be turned away. This last reason was used to expel the New York mobster Meyer Lansky in the 1970s.

'Was Meyer Lansky more dangerous than these people?' Goldschmidt asked.

THE MAKING OF A KILLER

Born to an Orthodox Jewish family in Brooklyn, New York, Baruch Kappel Goldstein studied to become a doctor. He also joined the Jewish Defense League, a militant Jewish organization founded by Rabbi Meir Kahane.

In 1981 he wrote a letter to the editor of the *New York Times*, warning that in Israel the Arab minority would outbreed the Israeli settlers, making them the majority. 'Ceding the "West Bank" to the "Palestinians" would, therefore, not solve the problem ... it would serve only to further jeopardize Israel's security and betray a Biblical trust.'

After emigrating to Israel, Goldstein formed a strong personal relationship with Rabbi Kahane. He served as a physician in the Israeli Defence Force, first as a conscript, then in the reserve forces. Following the end of his active duty, Goldstein worked as a physician and lived in the Kiryat Arba settlement near Hebron, where he served as an emergency doctor.

sources also said that some Palestinians may have been trampled to death in the headlong rush to escape the gunman's hail of bullets.

It was concluded that Goldstein had acted alone, firing about 100 rounds. , which is the number of casings that were retrieved from the floor of the mosque. Israeli officials counted 39 people killed at the mosque; the Palestinians gave a figure of 52, plus 70 wounded.

Beaten to death by the crowd

Goldstein was eventually cracked over the head with a fire extinguisher hurled by someone in the crowd. Then he was beaten to death. He had guessed this would be his fate. He had sent goodbye notes to the town council of Kiryat Arba where he lived and to a colleague who had worked with him at the clinic there, indicating that he would not return. To the co-worker he wrote, 'I enjoyed working as a doctor. Wishing for full redemption.'

Although Israeli Prime Minister Yitzhak Rabin condemned Goldstein, the attack set off riots and protests throughout the occupied territories. Another 19 Palestinians were killed by the Israeli Defence Forces within 48 hours of the massacre. The Israeli government set up a commission of inquiry to investigate the event. It found that Baruch Goldstein had acted alone in the planning and execution of the massacre, telling no one of his scheme. The report concluded that the massacre was 'a base and murderous act, in which innocent people bending in prayer to their maker were killed'.

Goldstein was praised as a martyr by some Jewish extremists in Hebron, and his gravesite became a site of pilgrimage for Israeli militants. A plaque near the grave read: 'To the holy Baruch Goldstein, who gave his life for the Jewish people, the Torah and the nation of Israel.' In 1999, after a law was passed that prohibited monuments to terrorists, the Israeli Supreme Court ruled that the shrine and prayer area set up near Goldstein's grave must be destroyed. They were razed by an Israeli Army bulldozer.

THOMAS HAMILTON

UK, 13 March 1996

The Dunblane massacre

On 13 March 1996 unemployed former shopkeeper and former Scout leader Thomas Watt Hamilton walked into the primary school in Dunblane, a tight-knit Scottish town a short drive northeast of Glasgow. He was armed with two 9mm Browning HP pistols and two Smith & Wesson .357 Magnum revolvers. The Brownings were loaded with armour-piercing full-metal-jacket and deadly hollow-point rounds. He was also carrying 743 cartridges. It was later reported that he had intended to turn up at the school at assembly, where all the children would be together, but was delayed by ice on the road.

After gaining entry to the school, 43-year-old Hamilton, wearing a woolly hat and earmuffs, made his way to the gymnasium and opened fire on a class of five- and six-year-olds. His first targets were the adults – possibly because they were a threat to him. Physical education teacher Eileen Harrild was hit in the chest, then as she put her arms up to protect her body, she was shot three more times in her arms and hand.

Mary Blake, a supervisory assistant, was next. She was shot in both legs and in the head. Then the 45-year-old gym teacher Gwen Mayor was shot six times. One of the bullets hit her in the right eye. She died instantly.

Terrified children

The gunman then turned his guns on the children, who by this time were running around, panicking and screaming. He killed 15 of them. Meanwhile, the wounded teachers Eileen Harrild and Mary Blake had crawled to the storeroom, which was in a blind spot from the door which the gunman had used to enter the gym. Some of the children had followed them. Several had been wounded. The two women were afraid that the children's crying would attract the gunman and tried to quieten them.

One victim was six-year-old Coll Austin. Initially shot in the foot, Coll was hopping towards the storeroom when he was shot again, in the arm and then in the

VICTIMS
Victoria Elizabeth Clydesdale, 5
Emma Elizabeth Crozier, 5
Melissa Helen Currie, 5
Charlotte Louise Dunn, 5
Kevin Allan Hasell, 5
Ross William Irvine, 5
David Charles Kerr, 5
Mhairi Isabel MacBeath, 5
Brett McKinnon, 6
Abigail Joanne McLennan, 5
Gwen Mayor, 45, schoolteacher
Emily Morton, 5
Sophie Jane Lockwood North, 5
John Petrie, 5
Joanna Caroline Ross, 5
Hannah Louise Scott, 5
Megan Turner, 5

back. He fell face down and saw one of his friends lying in a pool of blood, apparently staring blankly at him. As Coll lay there, he heard the gunman approach and saw his boots in front of him. Hamilton shot Coll again in the back and he slipped into a coma.

After about three minutes Hamilton left the gymnasium through the fire exit. In the playground outside he began shooting into a mobile classroom. A teacher had already realized that something was seriously wrong and told the children to hide under the tables. One pupil said: 'We heard these gunshots from the gym and looked round and thought he must be firing at a target or something, then he came out through a fire exit and started firing at our huts and we were all petrified.'

Most of the bullets became embedded in books and equipment, though one passed through a chair occupied by a child seconds before.

'Dived under my desk'

Eleven-year-old Steven Hopper was in a classroom near the gym. 'I looked over and saw the gunman,' he said. 'He was coming towards me, so I just dived under my desk when he turned and fired at us. It was pretty scary when he started firing at our classroom window because all the glass smashed in and I got hit by a piece.' Hamilton also fired at a group of children walking in a corridor, injuring another teacher. He then returned to the gym, where he put one of his revolvers into his mouth and pulled the trigger, killing himself instantly. In all, he had fired 109 times.

Jack Beattie, a senior consultant paediatrician, arrived with the medical team. 'We saw a large number of dead and injured children when we arrived in the gymnasium,' he said. 'There were a number of teachers comforting the children who were still alive and ambulance staff who had arrived before us. The children were very quiet. They were in shock both because of the injuries and because of the psychological shock.'

THE CULLEN INQUIRY

Following the massacre, an inquiry was set up to investigate the causes under Lord Cullen. It examined police reports and took evidence from those who had known Hamilton. It found that Hamilton had run some 16 boys' clubs, though he was not qualified to do so. Boys were forced to strip down to their swimming trunks so Hamilton could photograph them. Many of the pictures focused on the crotch area. Hamilton claimed that they were taken for advertising purposes, though he kept most of them at home, supposedly for his own enjoyment. However, Cullen found only two incidents that actively suggested that Hamilton was a paedophile, though even here the evidence was weak.

There was also evidence that Hamilton had planned the massacre some time in advance – as long as two years before. Certainly, six months before the shooting he bought more guns and ammunition, and upped his target practice. One nine-year-old member of one his clubs was regularly quizzed about the layout of Dunblane Primary School and its routine. However, the evidence on Hamilton's activities in the run-up to the massacre has been closed for 100 years to protect the identities of the children named in the reports.

THE MAKING OF A KILLER

Hamilton's motives were unknown. The pathologist Professor Anthony Busuttil, who performed the post-mortem on Hamilton and his victims, looked for a physical cause for the killer's behaviour. He looked for evidence of a brain tumour, alcohol, drugs, viral infection and even lead poisoning, but was unable to find any physical explanation. Professor Busuttil came to the conclusion that Hamilton's problems were based on unknown psychological factors.

Hamilton had had a disrupted childhood. By the time he was born on 10 May 1952 his parents were already divorced. They had only been married for two-and-half years and Hamilton never got to know his real father. His mother was herself adopted. At two Hamilton was adopted by his grandparents in Glasgow. They moved to Stirling, not far from Dunblane, when he was 12.

As a teenager, he became a member of the Boys Brigade and a rifle club. In his mid-20s he got a firearms licence and began collecting guns. He became an assistant Scout master, but after risking the lives of boys on winter expeditions he was forced to resign. He then began a number of boys' clubs in the area. He taught the youngsters how to shoot and took them on hunting expeditions. There were rumours of sadistic behaviour and he was accused of being a paedophile. The police investigated, but could not find enough evidence to prosecute – though a report recommended that his gun licence be revoked.

Hamilton complained that he was being victimized and alleged that there was a conspiracy against him. It seems that, in the Dunblane massacre, he sought to take his revenge on a community that strove to protect their children. However, no one who knew Hamilton saw anything odd about his behaviour in the run-up to the massacre. His mother saw him the night before and said there was no indication of what he was going to do the following day.

Twelve wounded children and three adults were rushed to hospital as soon as the emergency services arrived. One of these children was pronounced dead on arrival at the hospital. However, despite being wounded so severely four times, young Coll Austin was still alive and was rushed to Yorkhill Hospital in Glasgow. He had two bullets in his back. One had broken his ribs and collapsed both of his lungs. The other had exited through his head. Narrowly missing his brain, it had broken his jaw and fractured his cheekbone.

Coll's parents were told that his chances of survival were slim. However, after three days, he awoke from his coma. Though he had lost his sight and hearing on his right-hand side, after about a week Coll was well enough to go home and eventually recovered fully from his injuries.

Change in the law

Hamilton purchased his weapons legally. The Dunblane massacre led to a ban on the private ownership of handguns in the UK. Six days after the massacre, Hamilton's body was cremated in a private ceremony. The gymnasium where the massacre took place was demolished the following month, and within two years Dunblane Primary School was completely refurbished.

MARTIN
BRYANT

Australia, 28 April 1996

The Port Arthur massacre

Port Arthur, once one of Australia's most brutal penal settlements, is the top tourist attraction in Tasmania. By 1.30 p.m. on 28 April 1996 over 500 visitors were on the site. Business at the Broad Arrow Café had slowed after lunch but still some 60 people were finishing their meals or browsing in the gift shop when a young man with long blond hair entered. He was carrying a large blue duffel bag and sat on the balcony to eat his lunch. 'There's a lot of wasps about today,' he said to no one in particular. A few minutes later, he remarked that there were few Japanese tourists.

When he had finished his meal, he moved to the back of the café and set up a video camera on a vacant table. Then he unzipped the duffel bag. Producing an AR15 semi-automatic rifle, he shot Moh Yee Ng, a visitor from Malaysia, in the neck, killing him instantly. He swung the rifle from the hip and shot Soo Leng Chung, the man's companion, through the head. Next he shot Mick Sargent, grazing his scalp and knocking him to the floor. A fourth shot hit Sargent's girlfriend in the back of the head. In a matter of seconds, three people were dead.

The fusillade continued as the gunman shot at other customers and staff. Before he finished in the café he had killed 20 and wounded a further 15. Leaving the café, the gunman walked out into the crowded parking lot where there was some confusion. Hearing the shots, some people had started walking towards the café in the mistaken belief that a re-enactment was in progress. Others, who had seen the carnage, ran for cover, screaming warnings to anyone who would listen.

Tourists forced to take cover

The gunman opened fire once more, hitting several tourists. There was panic. He shot the driver of a tour bus and three passengers. Others took cover under the bus. The gunman saw them and calmly squatted down and shot them. Then he walked back to his car, a yellow Volvo 244GL saloon with a surfboard strapped to the roof, and drove off.

Three hundred metres away (328 yds) a young woman and her two children were walking beside the road. Pulling to a halt, the gunman fired two shots, killing the woman and the child she was carrying. The older child ran away and hid behind a tree. The gunman followed and killed her with a single shot.

He returned to his vehicle and drove another 200 metres (218 yds) towards the entrance where a gold-coloured BMW was parked. He shot the car's three occupants and dragged their bodies from the car. Then he transferred his baggage into the BMW and drove away.

A little way up the road he saw a couple in a white Toyota at a service station and stopped in front of it. He ordered the driver, Glenn Pears, to get out of the car and

VICTIMS

Winifred Joyce Aplin, 58

Walter John Bennett, 66

Nicole Louise Burgess, 17

Soo Leng Chung, 32

Elva Rhonda Gaylard, 48

Zoe Anne Hall, 28

Elizabeth Jayne Howard, 26

Mary Elizabeth Howard, 57

Mervyn John Howard, 55

Ronald Noel Jary, 71

Tony Vadivelu Kistan, 51

Leslie Dennis Lever, 53

Sarah Kate Loughton, 15

David Martin, 72

Noelene Joyce Martin, 69

Pauline Virjeana Masters, 49

Alannah Louise Mikac, 6

Madeline Grace Mikac, 3

Nanette Patricia Mikac, 36

Andrew Bruce Mills, 49

Peter Brenton Nash, 32

Gwenda Joan Neander, 67

Moh Yee Willing Ng, 48

Anthony Nightingale, 44

Mary Rose Nixon, 60

Glenn Roy Pears, 35

Russell James Pollard, 72

Janette Kathleen Quin, 50

Helene Maria Salzmann, 50

Robert Graham Salzmann, 58

Kate Elizabeth Scott, 21

Kevin Vincent Sharp, 68

Raymond John Sharp, 67

Royce William Thompson, 59

Jason Bernard Winter, 29

forced him into the boot of the BMW. The gunman then slammed the lid down and fired two shots through the driver's window, killing Pears's girlfriend Zoe Hall instantly. With the man locked in the boot, the gunman sped away towards a local guesthouse called Seascape Cottage.

On the way, the gunman saw another vehicle approaching and opened fire, but missed. The next vehicle was a four-wheel-drive jeep driven by a holidaying couple from Melbourne. One bullet tore into the bonnet; a second smashed the windscreen. More shots hit the side windows, showering the occupants with glass and hitting the woman driver in the forearm. Her male companion leant over to drive the vehicle to safety, but the throttle cable was severed. A Ford saloon with two married couples on board was also hit by a hail of bullets. Although bleeding profusely, the driver reached the point where the jeep had stopped and rescued the occupants.

Death at the guesthouse

After parking the BMW outside Seascape Cottage, the gunman moved his guns inside. Then he released Pears from the boot and took him into the guesthouse where he was handcuffed to the banister. Then the gunman returned to the car, poured petrol over it and set it alight.

Constable Paul Hyland had received an emergency call from Port Arthur and was on his way there when he saw several damaged vehicles and stopped to investigate. It was then that he saw smoke billowing from the BMW parked in front of Seascape Cottage. More

THE MAKING OF A KILLER

Martin Bryant had an IQ equivalent to that of an 11-year-old. On leaving school, he was assessed for a disability pension by a psychiatrist who wrote: 'Cannot read or write. Does a bit of gardening and watches TV ... Only his parents' efforts prevent further deterioration. Could be schizophrenic and parents face a bleak future with him.'

At 19 Bryant was befriended by a wealthy eccentric recluse, Helen Harvey, who was 35 years his senior. He did odd jobs for her and, after her mother died, moved into her mansion. His mood grew darker and his temper flared. At his next pension assessment, the interviewer recorded: 'Father protects him from any occasion which might upset him as he continually threatens violence ... Martin tells me he would like to go around shooting people. It would be unsafe to allow Martin out of his parents' control.'

In 1992 Harvey died in a car accident. Bryant was also injured. It was thought that he had lunged for the steering wheel, something he had done before. Bryant was the sole beneficiary of Harvey's will and inherited assets worth $550,000. Then Bryant's father died in suspicious circumstances.

Bryant developed a grudge against David and Noelene Martin, the owners of the nearby Seascape Cottage guesthouse which Bryant's father had wanted to buy. He blamed them for his father's death and it is thought that he went to Seascape Cottage and killed them before he headed for Port Arthur.

policemen turned up just as the BMW exploded in a burst of flames, sending them diving for cover. Then they came under fire from the cottage.

As it was thought that the gunman had at least three hostages – Glenn Pears and David and Noelene Martin, who owned Seascape Cottage – the police held back. Information came though that it was believed the lone gunman was Martin Bryant, a 28-year-old resident of New Town. He was known to be carrying AR15 and FN semi-automatic rifles. He also had access to more firearms that the Martins kept in Seascape Cottage. There was little cover around the cottage, so an assault was ruled out. Instead Special Operations Group and a negotiation team were called in. They arrived shortly after darkness fell.

Negotiations went on for the next six hours. Bryant's only demand was a ride on an army helicopter to the airport. Eventually, contact was lost when the batteries on the cordless phone that Bryant was using went flat. During the negotiations Glenn Pears was killed. The Martins, as was later discovered, were already dead.

The following morning Bryant set fire to the guesthouse and attempted to escape in the confusion. At 8.25 a.m. he ran from the building, his clothes ablaze. The police rushed to put the flames out. Bryant was arrested. He had burns to his back and buttocks and was taken to the Royal Hobart Hospital.

When the case came to court, Bryant initially pleaded not guilty, but was persuaded to change his plea. He was given 35 life sentences, one for each murder, plus 735 years for related crimes. In theory he will have to serve 1,035 years before he is eligible for parole.

ERIC HARRIS
& DYLAN
KLEBOLD

USA, 20 April 1999

The Columbine High School massacre

L 11:57:20-63 AM 04

At 11.10 a.m. on 20 April 1999 19-year-old Eric Harris drove into the student car park at Columbine High School in Littleton, a suburb of Denver, Colorado, and parked in a space assigned to another student, his co-conspirator 17-year-old Dylan Klebold. They avowedly hated Jews, gays and blacks and had chosen 20 April for their massacre as it was Hitler's birthday. Getting out of his car, Harris spoke to a fellow student, telling him to flee because he liked him. He was the only person they would willingly spare that day.

A few minutes later Harris and Klebold walked into the school cafeteria, carrying two large duffel bags. They put them on the floor beside other students' backpacks and bags. Each duffel bag contained an 8-kg propane bomb timed to explode at 11.17 a.m. when there would be nearly 500 students in the cafeteria. They returned to their car to watch the explosion and shoot down anyone who managed to escape the blast.

At around the same time there was a small explosion in a field a few minutes from the school. Bombs had been placed there as a diversionary tactic. However, only one had gone off, setting fire to the grass. Harris and Klebold were inexpert bomb-makers and the bombs in the cafeteria failed to go off too.

At 11.19 a.m. the couple were seen standing together at the top of the west steps, the highest point on the campus. They were wearing black trench coats, which hid 9mm semi-automatics, and were carrying a duffel bag and a backpack. A witness heard one of them say: 'Go! Go!'

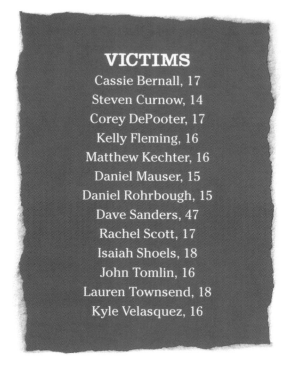

VICTIMS

Cassie Bernall, 17
Steven Curnow, 14
Corey DePooter, 17
Kelly Fleming, 16
Matthew Kechter, 16
Daniel Mauser, 15
Daniel Rohrbough, 15
Dave Sanders, 47
Rachel Scott, 17
Isaiah Shoels, 18
John Tomlin, 16
Lauren Townsend, 18
Kyle Velasquez, 16

College hitmen

They pulled shotguns out of their bags and began shooting. The first shots hit Rachel Scott and Richard Castaldo who were eating their lunch on the grass. Lance Kirklin, Sean Graves and Daniel Rohrbough were hit by gunfire as they came out of the cafeteria. Five other students, who had been sitting on the grass, tried to run and were shot at. Michael Johnson suffered gunshot wounds but managed to take cover in the athletic storage shed with three others, but Mark Taylor was gunned down.

Klebold descended the stairs to the cafeteria and shot Daniel Rohrbough again at close range, killing him. He also shot Lance Kirklin a second time, but Kirklin miraculously survived. Meanwhile Harris shot at Anne Marie Hochhalter, hitting her numerous times. The two gunmen then lit explosive devices and threw them, one of them shouting: 'This is awesome!'

'Today the world's going to come to an end. Today's the day we die.'

At 11.24 a.m. teacher Dave Sanders and staff members Jon Curtis and Jay Gallatine went into the cafeteria and told the students to take cover under the lunch tables. Meanwhile teacher Patti Nielson saw two male students carrying what she assumed were toy guns. She thought that they were part of a school video and was going to tell them to keep the noise down when Harris fired into the doorway. Nielson was showered with shards of glass, which cut her knee, forearm and shoulder. Student Brian Anderson was also cut by flying glass. The two managed to flee into the school library where they told other students to hide under the tables.

Harris and Klebold were distracted by the arrival of Deputy Paul Gardner, siren wailing. As Gardner stepped out of his patrol car, Harris fired ten shots at him before his rifle jammed. Gardner returned fire. Seconds later Harris was spraying bullets around again, before he retreated into the school.

Jefferson County Deputies Scott Taborsky and Paul Smoker arrived to see Gardner brandishing his service revolver. A gunman carrying a semi-automatic rifle appeared. Another opened fire from a window, then disappeared. Shots were heard inside the building.

THE TRENCH COAT MAFIA

Harris and Klebold were members of the Trench Coat Mafia, disaffected youths who complained they were harassed by the school's athletes – the 'jocks'. Some worked at Blackjack Pizza with Harris and Klebold. Others knew them from school. They wore black trench coats. In the senior class photograph from 1999 several members – including Harris and Klebold – posed as if pointing weapons at the camera. Some had seen the pipe bombs Harris and Klebold had made, but denied knowing what they were planning.

Laughing killers

In the main north hallway, Harris and Klebold began firing at students, laughing. Student Stephanie Munson fled towards the exit. She was hit in the ankle, but managed to escape. Dave Sanders had led the students from the cafeteria to safety. He was on the second level when he saw a gunman coming down the hallway. As he turned to run away he was shot. He managed to crawl to the science block where two Eagle Scouts gave him first aid. Despite their efforts, Sanders died.

Harris and Klebold set off pipe bombs in the hallway. They threw two more down the stairwell into the cafeteria and shot up the hallway outside the library. Inside the library they told the students to get up. One student was killed and another injured by

THE TAPES

Harris and Klebold left a series of videotapes that made it apparent that they had been planning the massacre for some time. They aimed to blow up a sizeable part of the school with hundreds of students in it. It took the authorities several days to find and defuse all the bombs they had planted. After reducing the school to rubble, they planned to blow up a plane over New York City and wanted a movie retelling their story to be made by Steven Spielberg or Quentin Tarantino.

The couple mentioned their obsession with the video game *Doom*, but the only stated motive for the killings was to get their own back on the 'jocks'. In the end, the killings were blindly indiscriminate.

In the tapes, Harris and Klebold exonerated their parents. Klebold said his mother and father had been 'great parents' who had taught him 'self-awareness, self-reliance … I always appreciated that'. He added: 'I am sorry I have so much rage.'

'It fucking sucks to do this to them,' said Harris, adding: 'There's nothing you guys could've done to prevent this.' Quoting Shakespeare's *The Tempest*, he said: 'Good wombs hath borne bad sons.' Just before they set off for Columbine, Harris and Klebold made one final videotape, saying goodbye. Klebold said: 'It's a half hour before Judgement Day … I didn't like life very much … I just know I'm going to a better place than here.'

Harris concluded: 'I know my mom and dad will be in shock and disbelief … I can't help it … That's it. Sorry. Goodbye.'

In another tape Harris and Klebold thanked Mark Manes and Phillip Duran for supplying them with the weapons they needed. Manes pleaded guilty to selling an Intrac TEC-9 9mm pistol to Klebold, a juvenile. He also supplied 100 9mm rounds to Harris on the night before the massacre and handled one of their sawn-off shotguns. He was sentenced to six years.

Phillip Duran, who worked with Harris and Klebold at Blackjack Pizza, was charged with brokering the deal with Manes and handling a sawn-off shotgun during target practice. He was sentenced to four-and-a-half years in prison. Both Duran and Manes denied any knowledge of Harris and Klebold's plans.

flying splinters of wood, before Harris and Klebold began a gunfight with the police out of the windows. Then they turned their attention to the students in the library, killing another nine and injuring 11 more.

After that they made their way down the hallway to the science block. On the way, they shot into empty rooms, but made no attempt to get into the locked classrooms where students hid. They rained down more pipe bombs into the cafeteria, though everyone who had been there had already been killed, escaped or taken cover – 17 were hiding in the kitchen. They then went down into the cafeteria and made one more attempt to detonate the propane bombs hidden in duffel bags there.

They managed to start a small fire, which set the sprinklers off, and shot at the paramedics who were trying to attend to the wounded outside. This started another gunfight with the police. By 12.06 p.m., when the first SWAT team turned up, Harris and Klebold were already dead. They had shot themselves shortly after that last exchange of fire from the library window. But it was not until 4.45 p.m. that the SWAT team had cleared the school and confirmed that the two suspects were dead.

MARK ORRIN BARTON

The day-trader

Atlanta day-trader Mark Barton had been on a losing streak and on Thursday 29 July 1999 he attended an appointment with the management at Momentum Securities to put up $50,000 in cash so he could continue trading. Two days before he had lost his trading privileges for the second time in three months. He had been unable to meet a margin call – a brokerage firm's demand that a customer cover a debt caused by falling stock prices – and the cheque he had written had bounced. He had lost a total of over $100,000 in the previous two months.

Brokerage firms such as Momentum Securities provided trading terminals equipped with high-speed data connections that allowed day-traders like Barton to make thousands of transactions a day – making spectacular profits or catastrophic losses. Despite his reverses, Barton seemed to be in good spirits. No one suspected that he was carrying two guns.

'About to get a lot worse'

After about 20 minutes of small talk, Barton whipped out a Colt .45 and a 9mm semi-automatic. It was a bad trading day, he said with a smile, and it was about to get a lot worse. Then he began systematically shooting the people around him. Traders scrambled for the exits as bullets flew past them. By the time the police arrived, four people were already dead and many more wounded, but Barton was nowhere to be seen.

He had walked across the street – past the police – to the All-Tech Investment Group, another brokerage firm where he traded. He greeted the staff cheerfully and in a normal manner and walked directly towards the manager's office, where he commiserated about the Dow Jones' 200-point slide. No one in the office was yet aware of the horrific events that had happened at Momentum Securities across the street only minutes earlier.

A few minutes after Barton walked into the office, five shots rang out and the manager and his secretary lay on the floor, seriously wounded. Barton then made his

> ## VICTIMS
> Leigh Ann Vandiver Barton, 27, wife of Mark Barton
> Matthew David Barton, 11, son of Mark Barton
> Mychelle Elizabeth Barton, 8, daughter of Mark Barton
> Russell J. Brown, 42
> Dean Delawalla, 52
> Joseph J. Dessert, 60
> Kevin Dial, 38
> Jamshid Havash, 45
> Vadewattee Muralidhara, 44
> Edward Quinn, 58
> Allen Charles Tenenbaum, 48
> Scott A. Webb, 30

way towards the main trading room with a gun in each hand, shooting everyone he saw. Hearing gunshots, 53-year-old Nell Jones looked up from her computer. 'I was the first person who looked into his eyes,' she said. Barton was just three metres (10 ft) away when he raised a pistol and fired, missing her forehead by centimetres and hitting her terminal. As he went on firing, he was, she said, 'very calm, very determined, showing no feeling'. However, he made one ghoulish aside. As he left All-Tech's office, he said: 'I hope this doesn't ruin your trading day.' By then, five more people lay dead and many more were injured. Again, Barton managed to leave the building unnoticed by the police and disappeared on foot into a wooded area. No one knew where he went.

MORE MURDERS?

Barton's first wife Debra and her mother Eloise Spivey were killed in a lakeside trailer where they were spending Labor Day in 1993. They were hacked to death with an axe-like implement that was never found. The police immediately suspected Barton. He was already having an affair with Leigh Ann and, a few months before, had told her that he would soon be free to marry her.

Leigh Ann moved in less than a week after his first wife was killed. The police found traces of blood in his car, but not enough to prosecute. Barton refused to give a DNA sample or take a lie-detector test.

His second marriage was no happier than his first and, at the age of two-and-a-half, his daughter Mychelle complained to a care worker that her father had sexually molested her.

Shortly before Debra died, Barton had taken out a $600,000 life assurance policy on her. Given the police's suspicions, the insurance company refused to pay up. However, fearing that a jury would sympathize with the plight of the children, the company eventually settled for $450,000, with $150,000 going into a trust fund for the children. Barton blew the remaining $300,000 day-trading. Despite Barton's denial in his final letter, the police continued to believe that he had killed his first wife and mother-in-law.

'Please take care of him'

After they had identified Barton as a suspect the police headed to the apartment in the Stockbridge suburb of Atlanta that he shared with his second wife Leigh Ann and the two children from his first marriage. When they arrived, the police found the bodies of Barton's two children laid side-by-side in their beds and neatly wrapped in blankets with only their faces showing.

On top of the boy was a video game and a handwritten note that read: 'I give you Matthew David Barton, my son, my buddy, my life. Please take care of him.' There was a teddy bear on the girl's body and similar note that read: 'I give you Mychelle Elizabeth Barton, my daughter, my sweetheart, my life, please take care of her.'

Another note on the coffee table – this time written on a computer and printed out – directed the police to Leigh Ann's body, which was to be found in the master bedroom covered with a blanket. The police eventually found her body in the closet. It also had a note on it similar to the others that said: 'I give you my wife Leigh Ann Barton, my honey, my precious love. Please take care of her. I will love her forever.'

THE NOTE ON THE COFFEE TABLE

July 29, 1999, 6:38 a.m.

To Whom It May Concern:

Leigh Ann is in the master bedroom closet under a blanket. I killed her on Tuesday night. I killed Matthew and Mychelle Wednesday night.

There may be similarities between these deaths and the death of my first wife, Debra Spivey. However, I deny killing her and her mother. There's no reason for me to lie now. It just seemed like a quiet way to kill and a relatively painless way to die.

There was little pain. All of them were dead in less than five minutes. I hit them with a hammer in their sleep and then put them face down in a bathtub to make sure they did not wake up in pain. To make sure they were dead. I am so sorry. I wish I didn't. Words cannot tell the agony. Why did I?

I have been dying since October. I wake up at night so afraid, so terrified that I couldn't be that afraid while awake. It has taken its toll. I have come to hate this life and this system of things. I have come to have no hope. I killed the children to exchange them five minutes of pain for a lifetime of pain. I forced myself to do it to keep them from suffering so much later. No mother, no father, no relatives. The fears of the father are transferred to the son. It was from my father to me and from me to my son. He already had it and now to be left alone. I had to take him with me.

I killed Leigh Ann because she was one of the main reasons for my demise as I planned to kill the others. I really wish I hadn't killed her now. She really couldn't help it and I love her so much anyway.

I know that Jehovah will take care of all of them in the next life. I'm sure the details don't matter. There is no excuse, no good reason. I am sure no one would understand. If they could, I wouldn't want them to. I just write these things to say why.

Please know that I love Leigh Ann, Matthew and Mychelle with all of my heart. If Jehovah is willing, I would like to see all of them again in the resurrection, to have a second chance.

You should kill me if you can.

Mark O. Barton

The body count now lay at 12 dead and 22 injured. Nearly five hours after Barton had first disappeared from All-Tech he was seen at a shopping mall in Kennesaw, 20 minutes from Atlanta, where he threatened a young girl. She managed to run away from him and call the police. Barton seized the opportunity, quickly jumped into his van and drove away.

Witnesses gave a description to the police and Barton's van was soon followed by a swarm of unmarked police cars. Not realizing he was by now being tailed, Barton pulled into a petrol station in Acworth, ten minutes' drive to the northeast. The police pounced and within moments had surrounded his van. Brandishing their guns, they ordered Barton to get out of his vehicle. At this point Barton simply turned one of his own guns on himself and blew his brains out.

'I don't plan to live very much longer, just long enough to kill as many of the people that greedily sought my destruction'

ABBAS AL-BAQIR ABBAS

Sudan, 8 December 2000

The Jarafa mosque massacre

It was a Friday night during Ramadan at about 9 p.m. when 33-year-old lone gunman Abbas al-Baqir Abbas burst into the al-Sunna al-Mohammediyya Mosque in Jarafa, on the outskirts of the city of Omdurman in the Sudan, with an AK-47 assault rifle. He began shooting at the people who were at prayer, instantly killing at least 20 worshippers and wounding many more. 'There was blood all over the place, people were terrified,' said one worshipper.

According to witnesses, Abbas avoided targeting the women's section of the mosque and told a fleeing woman that he was only shooting men. When he refused to surrender, there was a brief shootout with the police and Abbas was killed. Over 33 were wounded in the attack, among them a police officer. Ambulances and private cars were used to rush the wounded to hospital. Some were in a critical condition and at least two of the injured later died of their wounds.

The police insisted that Abbas acted alone, dismissing reports that shots were fired from three different directions. Witnesses said that there had been at least three attackers dressed in *djellabas*, but all of them except Abbas had fled before the police arrived. There were also reports that, after the mosque had been attacked, the gunman went on a rampage through the village. Higher casualty figures were also reported. They ranged up to as many as 27 people killed and 53 wounded. An angry crowd demanding revenge gathered outside Omdurman University Hospital where the casualties were taken.

> "There was blood all over the place. People were terrified."
> Worshipper

The entire male population of the village turned out the following day to dig a mass grave, as Islamic tradition requires the dead to be buried within a day. Bodies were carried to the graveyard wrapped in blankets on a bedstead. Newspapers said that 18 bodies had been identified and that the authorities were due to carry out funerals for the other two Muslims, but it was not clear if they were buried in the same funeral.

Religious fanaticism

Abbas al-Baqir Abbas was from Al-Dasis in the northern part of Sudan's Al Jazirah region. His uncle said that his mother had left their home due to his religious fanaticism and that he beat his sister, accusing her of infidelity. He studied economics at Tripoli University, but was forced to leave Libya when the authorities feared that the Islamist groups he led threatened state security. Later he served in Sudan's Popular Defence Forces, undergoing military training to fight the anti-government rebels waging a 17-year civil war in the southern part of the county.

Abbas was a member of a Muslim extremist group, Takfir wal-Hijra, which means 'Atonement and Self-Denial'. Originating in Egypt, it believes that the Sharia, or Islamic

CHECHNYA

Ahmed Bragimov was acting alone when he went on a shooting spree on a sunny day in the Chechen town of Mekenskaya as the Russian army rolled into Chechnya. He targeted only Russians, survivors said, vowing to kill as many people as possible before Russian troops arrived to seize the town.

Bragimov shot and killed at least 34 people, leaving their bodies lying in the muddy streets or huddled in doorways. There is no evidence that he was working on orders of Chechen guerrillas who were fighting Russian troops in the breakaway republic. 'He was a killer and a thief, just as they all are,' said one Russian in Mekenskaya. 'The Chechens are all bandits. They would all kill us if they could.'

Another resident, Larisa Chikova, recalled how she and others hid from Bragimov as he moved through Mekenskaya killing people on 8 October 1999. 'He wasn't a Wahhabist,' she said. 'He just hated Russians. They all feel that way about Russians.'

Bragimov was caught by townspeople and beaten to death.

law, that prevails in Sudan should be imposed by force. The pacifist Ansar al-Sunna – Supporters of the Rules of the Prophet – whose members were victims of the massacre, do not believe this, though their movement is linked to the hard-line Wahhabi sect, the dominant religious force in Saudi Arabia. The dispute between the two sects had caused earlier shootings.

Sentenced to death

On 4 February 1994 one Libyan and two Sudanese Islamists attacked another Ansar al-Sunna mosque in Al Thawra with assault rifles, injuring 15 and killing 19 people. Their leader, Mohammad Abdullah al-Khilaifi, was captured and sentenced to death. On 1 January 1996 one police officer and eight attackers were killed in a shootout in Kambo Ashara, when the gunmen tried to force villagers to convert. The same year an attack on the mosque in Jarafa had left 12 people dead. Then on 1 November 1997 people leaving a mosque in Arkawit were attacked by two members of Takfir wal-Hijra wielding knives. Two worshippers were killed and another ten wounded.

Once a member of Ansar al-Sunna, Abbas had left because of religious differences and joined Takfir wal-Hijra. It was said that he had repeatedly threatened members of Ansar al-Sunna with an attack similar to the one in 1994. This led to his arrest in 1998. He was detained for four months. He was arrested again a few months before the 2000 shooting, along with 20 other people suspected of being members of Takfir wal-Hijra. However, when they recanted and claimed they had left the group, they were released.

Previous threats

After the 2000 attack, the newspaper *Al-Rai Al-Aam* reported that Abbas al-Baqir Abbas had previously threatened the congregation with an attack similar to the one in 1994. The mosque's prayer leader, Beshir Ibrahim, told the *Akhbar Al-Yom* newspaper

TAKFIR WAL-HIJRA

Takfir wal-Hijra can be translated variously as 'Atonement and Self-Denial' or 'Repentance and Flight', though its fuller meaning is 'repent your sins and flee the sinful world'. The name was used in Egypt in the early 1970s by a violent offshoot of the Muslim Brotherhood.

Since then the name has periodically been used by groups in other Arab countries. It is known to have been active in Algeria and Jordan. In 1996 a group using the name was thought to have plotted to assassinate Osama bin Laden for being insufficiently radical. There was also thought to have been a link between Takfir wal-Hijra and the Madrid bombing in 2004.

The sect advocates armed battle against Jews, Christians and apostate Muslims to restore the unity of the Islamic world order under a Caliph who rules according to the Sharia law.

The group's warriors are allowed to disguise their true principles to blend in with Western society and destroy it from within. These warriors will then be martyrs in paradise after death.

that the assailant was well known in the village and had broken away from Ansar al-Sunna. The attack took place just three days before general elections in Sudan, which were being boycotted by numerous opposition groups. However, observers said the dispute between Takfir wal-Hijra and Ansar al-Sunna was purely religious and there was no connection between the attack and the presidential and parliamentary elections.

The day after the shooting the president of Sudan, Omar al-Bashir, visited the mosque to offer his condolences to relatives of the victims and assure them that legislation would be passed to control fanatical religious groups. He vowed 'to rectify laws in order to protect society from destructive and harmful ideas'.

Fallout from the massacre

In the wake of the massacre, police and security forces were deployed in Khartoum state in a large-scale campaign, ostensibly to prevent further violence. When Omar al-Bashir won the subsequent election, 65 leading members of Takfir wal-Hijra were arrested and the security laws were tightened, allowing suspects to be detained for up to six months. However, opposition parties accused President al-Bashir of cynically using the shooting at the Jarafa mosque as an excuse to curtail liberties and increase his power.

Al-Bashir has since come in for international condemnation. On 4 March 2009 the International Criminal Court issued an arrest warrant for him on two counts of war crimes and five counts of crimes against humanity over the campaign of murder, rape and deportation in Darfur. However, it was ruled that there was insufficient evidence to prosecute him for genocide.

In 2010, al-Bashir won the presidential election with 68 per cent of the vote. He had hoped a win in legitimate polls would help him defy the ICC warrant, but remains the only sitting head of state wanted by the court.

DIPENDRA BIR BIKRAM SHAH

Nepal, 1 June 2001

The death of a dynasty

On the evening of 1 June 2001 there was a party in the Narayanhiti Palace in Kathmandu. As was the custom in the Nepalese royal family, the only people in attendance were royals. No bodyguards or servants were allowed. Twenty-nine-year-old Crown Prince Dipendra Bir Bikram Shah of Nepal offered to pour drinks. The Queen Mother was with her friends in the sitting room, while the younger crowd hung out around the bar and CD player in the billiard room.

As the evening drew on Crown Prince Dipendra got so drunk that he was 'stammering and falling down,' according Rajiv Raj Shahi, son-in-law of King Birendra's brother Dhirendra. The Crown Prince 'misbehaved' with a guest and was told to leave the party by his father, the king. Shahi, along with Dipendra's brothers, Paras and Niranjan, escorted him to his room.

Despite the behaviour of his son, King Birendra was in good humour. Drinking a cola, he was enjoying the court gossip and got involved in chitchat about cholesterol and gout. Then the mood turned serious. After about an hour, Dipendra returned to the billiard room dressed in combat fatigues. He was carrying a Heckler & Koch MP5, a machine pistol used by the Special Forces, and an M16. Dipendra fired a single shot into the ceiling before turning the gun on King Birendra. 'Dipendra just looked at his father. He said nothing and squeezed the trigger once,' said Ravi Shumshere Rana, Dipendra's 77-year-old uncle, who was standing next to the king when he was shot.

'I instinctively plugged my ears with my fingers and closed my eyes,' recalled Maheshwar Kumar Singh, another of the king's brothers-in-law. Opening his eyes, he found the king 'had a very strange look on his face, and then he began to lean to the right'.

'The king stood there for a few seconds after the firing and then slowly he sat down on the ground,' Rana recalled. Blood appeared on the king's right shoulder and began to spread. It was about this time that the king finally spoke. He said, '*Ke gareko?*' ('What have you done?')

Shahi was a military doctor and ran to the king, pressing his coat to his neck to staunch the bleeding. The king said

> ## VICTIMS
> King Birendra, 55, father
> Queen Aishwarya, 51, mother
> Prince Nirajan, 23, brother
> Princess Shruti, 24, sister
> Dhirendra, 50, uncle
> Princess Jayanti, 44, King Birendra's cousin
> Princess Shanti, 59, aunt
> Princess Sharada, 53, aunt
> Kumar Khadga, 58, Princess Sharada's husband

KING GYANENDRA

As king, Gyanendra dismissed the government and assumed full executive powers in an attempt to quash the Maoist guerrillas who had taken over much of the country. However, the confrontation reached a stalemate. The Maoists declared a unilateral ceasefire in September 2005. Under pressure from the movement for democracy, King Gyanendra agreed to cede sovereign power to the people. Nepal was declared a republic and Gyanendra was deposed. On 28 May 2008 the Maoists formed a coalition government and gave the king 15 days to vacate the Narayanhiti Palace, now a museum, and the reign of the Shah dynasty ended after nearly 450 years.

he had also been shot in the stomach. According to Shahi, Dipendra shot his father and an aunt several times during the carnage.

Prince Dhirendra tried stopping the Crown Prince but was shot in the chest at point-blank range. At that point Dipendra went wild, raking the room with indiscriminate gunfire. Then the Crown Prince left the room, only to return with a fatigue hat pulled low over his eyes so they were barely visible. He was walking steadily. This time he shot two uncles and his aunt, among others, and left the room again. He returned several times to finish the job.

On one occasion Shahi had to jump sideways as Dipendra veered towards him, then he managed to escape through a window and told some courtiers to call for ambulances. Despite the confusion there was no doubt about who the perpetrator was. Maheshwar Prasad Singh, who saved himself by diving for cover during the shooting, said: 'I'm very sorry to say this, but it was done by Dipendra.'

Royal family wiped out

'What motivated him to do this I am not sure,' said Shahi later. 'Had it not been for Prince Paras probably there would not have been so many survivors.'

Prince Paras had been in a corner of the billiard room, in front of a group of princesses. Eyewitnesses said that Paras saved at least three members of the royal family, including two children, by pulling a sofa over them. When Dipendra returned after a minute, he strode up to the five wounded or dead relatives, including the king, and fired at them again, at point-blank range, and then targeted his sister Shruti as she bent over her injured husband. The final time he returned, he pumped bullets into those he had already shot. Then Dipendra turned his gun towards Paras. Paras shouted, '*Nai, Dai! Nai, Dai!* (No, Brother! No, Brother!)' He didn't fire.

Dipendra then went out to the garden where his mother, Queen Aishwarya, and Prince Niranjan confronted him. Dipendra shot them both dead. The spree ended when Dipendra shot himself on a small bridge over a stream running through the palace. He died in hospital three days later.

At first the Nepalese government claimed that the shooting was an accident. The late king's younger brother Prince Gyanendra, who was appointed regent, issued a statement through the official media. It said: 'According to the information received by

THE MAKING OF A KILLER

Born on 27 June 1971, Dipendra was declared heir apparent to the throne of Nepal the following year. He received his early education at Budhanilkantha School in Kathmandu. He then went to Eton College in England, where he was disciplined for selling alcohol.

After Eton, Dipendra attended Tribhuvan University in Nepal and later joined the Military Academy at Kharipati. He studied for his master's degree at Tribhuvan University and was a PhD student there too.

In 1990 he became colonel-in-chief of the Royal Nepalese Army. He was also the patron of the National Sports Council, Royal Nepal Golf Club and Nepal Olympics Committee. He was known to have been skilled in karate and wrote poetry.

us, members of the royal family were seriously injured in an accidental firing from an automatic weapon.' However few believed that so many could have been killed in an accidental shooting.

Rumours then circulated that Crown Prince Dipendra had shot the victims during a family dinner at the palace after a row over his choice of bride. He wanted to marry 22-year-old Devyani Rana, who was half Indian, but his mother, Queen Aishwarya, was firmly opposed. However, neither Shahi nor Singh, nor indeed Rana, saw any indication that there had been a family row before the incident which might have set Dipendra off. Rana also denied that Dipendra was drunk, saying that when Dipendra had brought him a drink, he seemed sober and even claimed not to be drinking because there was no Famous Grouse whisky.

Later Paras said that there was another factor involved. The Crown Prince was frustrated that his father had rejected a planned arms deal which Dipendra had hoped would earn him about $1 million in kickbacks. 'His father, His Majesty, did not agree,' said Paras. 'I know that they argued over it. Dipendra was frustrated. He wasn't happy. He told me. That, to me, was the real trigger.'

According to Paras, Dipendra planned to use the money to elope with Devyani Rana. 'I think he was already making plans for the possibility that he would have to leave the country suddenly if things didn't work out for him. I think this was his back-up plan,' Paras said.

Three-day reign

Dipendra's self-inflicted shot to the head in the palace gardens put him into a coma. The Nepalese nation was in a state of shock. While lingering in this state in hospital he was nevertheless proclaimed king, as the constitution decreed. He reigned for just three days. After he died, Prince Gyanendra, who subsequently took the throne, confirmed that it was Dipendra who had been responsible for the massacre though, under the constitution, he could not have been charged with murder even had he survived. A full investigation by two Supreme Court judges also found that Dipendra, alone, was responsible. However, some thought that Gyanendra was behind the massacre.

SEUNG-HUI CHO

USA, 16 April 2007

The Virginia Tech massacre

Around 6.45 a.m. on 16 April 2007 23-year-old Virginia Tech student Seung-Hui Cho was seen near the entrance to West Ambler Johnston Hall, a co-ed residence at the college that housed 894 students. He was carrying two guns – a 9mm Glock 19 and a .22-calibre Walther P22. He went to the room of 19-year-old freshman Emily Hilscher. Not long after 7.15 a.m., shots were heard. Ryan Clark, a 22-year-old senior, heard the shots and went to investigate. He too was shot and killed. Cho went back to his dorm room in Harper Hall two minutes' walk away.

While the emergency medical service units rushed to the scene of the killing, Cho changed out of his bloodstained clothes and logged on to his computer to delete his email and wipe out his account. He then removed the hard drive and disposed of it, along with his mobile phone, probably in the campus pond, though they were never found. It appears that he also planned to dispose of the handguns as the serial numbers had been filed off.

Less than two hours after the murder of Hilscher and Clark, Cho was seen at a post office off campus where he mailed a package to NBC News in New York. Inside the package were pictures of Cho brandishing his guns, two rambling letters, and videos Cho had shot of himself. In them, he railed against society and how it had ill-treated him. He also mentioned the Columbine High School killers by name, indicating that he too craved fame through mass killing.

> 'You forced me into a corner and gave me only one option ... You loved inducing cancer in my head, terror in my heart and ripping my soul all this time'

A gifted loner

As a child in South Korea Seung-Hui Cho was plagued with health problems. He was extremely quiet and sweet natured, but had few friends. When he was eight, his parents moved to the USA in the hope of improving their children's educational opportunities. Cho and his older sister spoke no English and became isolated. Within two years they had learned English, but Cho could not read and write Korean, which was used at home.

Cho spoke little at home and, at school, he would not interact with other children. He went into therapy. By eighth grade, his therapist feared that he might be suicidal. After Columbine, there were fears that he might do the same. However, he was gifted in science and mathematics, and it was clear that he should go to college. A counsellor urged that he be sent to a small college close to home, but Cho was determined to go to Virginia Tech. Once there, he remained withdrawn.

He started stalking female students. The police warned him to stop. Instead he turned to text messaging, emails and Facebook. One recipient grew fearful and called the police. Cho was found to be mentally ill but, as he did not seem to be a danger to himself or others, he was not hospitalized. On the night before the massacre, Cho made his regular Sunday call to his parents. They suspected nothing.

VICTIMS

Ross Alameddine, 20
Jamie Bishop, 35
Brian Bluhm, 25
Ryan Clark, 22
Austin Cloyd, 18
Jocelyne Couture-Nowak, 49
Daniel Perez Cueva, 21
Kevin Granata, 45
Matthew Gwaltney, 24
Caitlin Hammaren, 19
Jeremy Herbstritt, 27
Rachael Hill, 18
Emily Hilscher, 19
Jarrett Lane, 22
Matthew La Porte, 20
Henry Lee, 20
Liviu Librescu, 76
G. V. Loganathan, 53
Partahi Lumbantoruan, 34
Lauren McCain, 20
Daniel O'Neil, 22
Juan Ortiz, 26
Minal Panchal, 26
Erin Peterson, 18
Michael Pohle Jr, 23
Julia Pryde, 23
Mary Karen Read, 19
Reema Samaha, 18
Waleed Shaalan, 32
Leslie Sherman, 20
Maxine Turner, 22
Nicole White, 20

Lethally equipped

On 16 April, after posting the package containing the photos, letters and videos, Cho headed for Norris Hall, which housed the Engineering, Science and Mechanics faculties. He was carrying a backpack that contained the two handguns, 19 rapid-loading magazines – almost 400 rounds of ammunition – and heavy chains that he used to secure the three main entrance doors.

At 9.40 a.m. Cho walked into room 206 where Professor G. V. Loganathan was teaching a class in hydrology. He shot and killed the professor. Without a word, he turned his gun on the class, killing nine of the 13 students in the room and injuring two others. Hearing the shots, Jocelyne Couture-Nowak, who was teaching French in room 211, asked student Colin Goddard to call the police on his mobile phone. Next, Cho moved across the hall to room 207, where Jamie Bishop was teaching German. Cho shot Bishop and students near the doorway, then moved down the aisle of the classroom, shooting others. Bishop and four others died, six were wounded.

In room 211, the students tried to barricade the door, but Cho pushed his way in. He shot Couture-Nowak and moved down the aisle, shooting the students. Again Cho said nothing. Colin Goddard was among the first to be shot, but another student, Emily Haas, picked up his mobile phone and stayed on the line while the shooting went on. Even though she was wounded twice in the head, she spoke quietly to the

LITERARY LIFE

Cho had ambitions to write a novel, but his ideas were rejected by New York publishers. He then got into heavy metal and stuck lyrics up on the walls around the dorm.

In poetry classes, he would appear wearing sunglasses and a hat pulled down over his face. When he read, his voice was inaudible. What he wrote was dark and he accused his classmates who ate meat of being complicit in the massacre of animals.

'If you despicable human beings who are all disgraces to the human race keep this up, before you know it you will turn into cannibals – eating little babies, your friends,' he wrote. 'I hope y'all burn in hell for mass murdering and eating all those little animals.' Cho's fellow students grew afraid of him and his teacher had him removed from her class. His written work continued in its dark vein. In one story, the protagonist, who is clearly based on himself, tells a 'gothic girl': 'I'm nothing. I'm a loser. I can't do anything. I was going to kill every god damn person in this damn school, swear to god I was, but I…couldn't. I just couldn't. Damn it I hate myself!' That autumn, he took a class called 'Contemporary Horror'.

After the massacre police found a suicide note in Cho's dorm room that included deprecatory comments about 'rich kids', 'debauchery' and 'deceitful charlatans'.

dispatcher, then closed her eyes and played dead. Hearing gunshots, students in room 205 lay on the floor and held the door closed with their feet. Cho fired through the door several times, but no one was injured.

Cho returned to room 207, but four survivors held the door closed. Nevertheless he managed to force the door open a little and fired about five shots around the door, before giving up. Returning to room 211, he walked up and down the aisles, shooting students at point-blank range. There were few places for the students to hide, except behind their desks which afforded little cover. Colin Goddard who was playing dead was shot twice more, though he survived. But the teacher and 11 students lay dead. Another six were wounded. Everyone in the entire class had fallen victim to Cho's bullets.

No place to hide

After reloading, Cho then tried to enter room 204 where Professor Liviu Librescu, a Holocaust survivor, was teaching mechanics. He braced his body against the door while students leapt through the windows. Shots fired through the door killed Librescu. Two students were then shot as they were making their escape through the window. In all, four students in the mechanics class were shot, one fatally.

The massacre continued for about 10 to 12 minutes. In that time, Cho had murdered 27 students and five faculty members. It was the highest death toll inflicted by a single killer in the USA. Another 15 were shot and survived, though the hollow-tipped bullets that Cho used caused terrible injuries. Six more were injured when they jumped from the windows. Cho ended the carnage by shooting himself in the head as the police closed in.

PEKKA-ERIC AUVINEN

Finland, 7 November 2007

The Jokela High School massacre

The Columbine High School massacre provoked copycat killings around the world – even as far away as Finland. At about 11.40 a.m. on 7 November 2007, 18-year-old student Pekka-Eric Auvinen walked into Jokela High School in Tuusula, southern Finland, and opened fire, cutting down his fellow pupils in the entrance way. The headmistress, 61-year-old Helena Kalmi, called the police, then ordered all students and teachers to barricade themselves in their classrooms.

Instead of seeking safety herself, Kalmi went out to confront the assailant. Auvinen forced her to her knees in the schoolyard, then shot her seven times in full view of pupils watching from a classroom window. The 43-year-old school nurse who went to the aid of injured students was shot and killed too.

Auvinen then began walking around the school, firing through classroom doors and shooting people at random. The victims sustained multiple injuries to head and upper body. Some had been shot up to 20 times. But Auvinen also pointed his gun at some people without shooting them. Shouting orders at students, he proclaimed that he was starting a revolution and urged the students to destroy school property. He doused the main corridor with petrol but he was unable to set it alight.

The police arrived at 11.55 a.m., but when they tried to start negotiations they were answered by a hail of bullets. Soon the school was surrounded by 100 officers, including a special operations unit. Even off-duty police officers turned up. In just 20 minutes, Auvinen had loosed off 69 rounds.

> 'I am prepared to fight and die for my cause. I, as a natural selector, will eliminate all who I see unfit, disgraces of human race and failures of natural selection.'

The 'antihuman humanist'

The attack ended at 12.24 p.m. when Auvinen turned the gun on himself. However, the police held off storming the school until 1.53 p.m., more than two hours after they had first been called. Auvinen was found in a school toilet unconscious but still alive. He was taken to Helsinki University Central Hospital, but died from his wounds that evening.

In their investigation, the police confirmed that Auvinen had been a victim of school bullying for years. Born locally, he described himself on his YouTube user page as 'a cynical existentialist, antihuman humanist, antisocial social Darwinist, realistic idealist and godlike atheist'. He had a conventional two-parent family. His father was a musician, his mother was a deputy on Tuusula municipal council. He also had an 11-year-old brother.

One of his teachers said he was above average academically and took an interest in history, philosophy and politics – particularly extreme right- and left-wing

PERSONAL PROFILE

So that people would know him a little better, Auvinen had posted a personal profile on the web. This read:

'**Occupation:** Unemployed Philosopher, Outcast
Companies: Human Race (evolved one step above though)
Interests and Hobbies: Existentialism, Freedom, Truth, Misanthropy, Social/Personality Psychology, Evolution Science, Political Incorrectness, Women, BDSM, Guns (I love you Catherine), Shooting, Computer Games, Sarcasm, Irony, Mass/Serial Killers, Macabre Art, Black Comedy, Absurdism
Movies and Shows: The Matrix, A View To A Kill, Falling Down, Natural Born Killers, Reservoir Dogs, Last Man Standing, Full Metal Jacket, Dr. Butcher MD (aka Zombie Holocaust), Saw 1-3, Lord Of War, The Deer Hunter, True Romance, The Untouchables, 28 Days Later, 28 Weeks Later, Idiocracy, They Live, Apocalypse Now, End Of Days, The Shining, The Dead Zone, Dr. Strangelove, House MD (TV), Monty Python (TV) Documentaries Relating To History
Music: KMFDM, Rammstein, Eisbrecher, Nine Inch Nails, Grendel, Impaled Nazarene, Macabre, Deathstars, The Prodigy, Combichrist, Godsmack, Slayer, Children Of Bodom, Alice Cooper, Sturmgeist, Suicide Commando, Hatebreed, Suffocation, Terrorizer
Books: Fahrenheit 451 (Bradbury), 1984 (Orwell), Brave New World (Huxley), The Republic (Plato), all works of Nietzsche'

movements. However, he had been on anti-depressants since he was 17. These sometimes induce suicidal tendencies as a side-effect in adolescents.

The massacre had not been long in the planning. Auvinen had only received his gun licence three weeks before the school shootings. He was a registered member of the Helsinki Shooting Club, but had only attended a single one-hour training session.

His weapon, a SIG Sauer Mosquito .22-calibre handgun, had been obtained legally and was registered to Auvinen on 19 October. Auvinen himself wanted to buy a more powerful Beretta 9mm pistol, but his application was rejected by police. In Finland the police usually require a hobby shooter to begin with a .22-calibre weapon.

An hour before the shooting, Auvinen uploaded a home-made video called the 'Jokela High School Massacre – 11/7/2007' to YouTube. KMFDM's song 'Stray Bullet' was used as background music. This track was also used on the website of Columbine High School shooter Eric Harris.

'Shock and awe'

There were earlier indications of what he had in mind. Weeks before the shootings, he had uploaded videos of himself shooting his new gun. Many of his other YouTube videos were about other shootings and violent incidents, including the Columbine High School massacre, the Waco siege, the Tokyo sarin gas attack and the 'shock and awe' bombing during the Iraq invasion.

A spokesman for the cyber-crime department of Helsinki police said that 'it's highly probable that there was some form of contact between Pekka-Eric

NATURAL SELECTION

Auvinen posted a manifesto on the Internet which aimed to explain his actions. Part of it read:

'You might ask yourselves, why did I do this and what do I want. Well, most of you are too arrogant and closed-minded to understand ... You will probably say me that I am "insane", "crazy", "psychopath", "criminal" or crap like that. No, the truth is that I am just an animal, a human, an individual, a dissident.

I have had enough. I don't want to be part of this fucked up society. Like some other wise people have said in the past, human race is not worth fighting for or saving ... only worth killing. But when my enemies will run and hide in fear when mentioning my name ... when the gangsters of the corrupted governments have been shot in the streets ... when the rule of idiocracy and the democratic system has been replaced with justice ... when intelligent people are finally free and rule the society instead of the idiocratic rule of majority ... in that great day of deliverance, you will know what I want.

Long live the revolution ... revolution against the system, which enslaves not only the majority of weak-minded masses but also the small minority of strong-minded and intelligent individuals! If we want to live in a different world, we must act. We must rise against the enslaving, corrupted and totalitarian regimes and overthrow the tyrants, gangsters and the rule of idiocracy. I can't alone change much but hopefully my actions will inspire all the intelligent people of the world and start some sort of revolution against the current systems. The system discriminating again nature and justice is my enemy. The people living in the world of delusion and supporting this system are my enemies.

I am ready to die for a cause I know is right, just and true ... even if I would lose or the battle would be only remembered as evil ... I will rather fight and die than live a long and unhappy life.

And remember that this is my war, my ideas and my plans. Don't blame anyone else for my actions than myself. Don't blame my parents or my friends. I told nobody about my plans and I always kept them inside my mind only. Don't blame the movies I see, the music I hear, the games I play or the books I read. No, they had nothing to do with this. This is my war: one man war against humanity, governments and weak-minded masses of the world! No mercy for the scum of the earth! HUMANITY IS OVERRATED! It's time to put NATURAL SELECTION & SURVIVAL OF THE FITTEST back on tracks!

"Justice renders to everyone his due."'

Auvinen and Dillon Cosey', a 14-year-old boy arrested the month before on suspicion of planning an attack on his school in a suburb of Philadelphia. Acting on a tip-off, the police found a 9mm semi-automatic rifle, handmade grenades, a .22 pistol and a .22 single-shot rifle at Cosey's home.

It was less than two weeks later that Auvinen, already a member of a shooting club, was buying his first gun – a .22 pistol – and expressing interest in a 9mm semi-automatic. The police did not believe this to have been a coincidence. The two youths were thought to have made contact through two MySpace groups, 'RIP Eric and Dylan' – a reference to Eric Harris and Dylan Klebold, who killed 12 schoolmates at Columbine – and 'Natural Selection'.

ISAAC ZAMORA

USA, 2 September 2008

'I kill for God'

At 2.19 p.m. on 2 September 2008 the police received a 911 call from Dennise Zamora, a resident of the small town of Alger in North Skagit County, Washington state. Deputy Anne Jackson was sent to investigate. At 2.50 p.m. she arrived at 19342 Bridle Place in Alger. When she did not check in with her dispatchers, other deputies were sent to investigate. They found Jackson dead outside the building, and the body of a man inside.

At 4.10 p.m. there were reports that a motorcyclist had been shot in the arm at a Shell filling station. Officers were in pursuit south down Interstate 5. Shots were exchanged and 42-year-old Washington State Trooper Troy Giddings was hit in the arm. The police then received word of a fatal collision at mile post 238 near the Bow Hill Creek Road exit of I-5. They found an SUV on the central reservation. The driver had been shot and killed.

At 4.30 p.m. 28-year-old Isaac Zamora drove up to the sheriff's office in Mount Vernon, Washington, and turned himself in. He said he was the killer and his spree, it seemed, had come to an end. However, the full extent of his rampage was yet to be revealed.

'Guilty, guilty, guilty, guilty'

At 5 p.m. one of Zamora's neighbours came home to find two workmen dead in her house at 19522 Silver Creek Drive. Zamora had also stabbed a 61-year-old man, who had escaped and run for help. Police found the dead body of a woman outside her house, and later also identified her husband, who had been shot but had managed to escape into the woods nearby. In all, six people were dead and four wounded.

Zamora already had a prison record and had only been released from jail on 6 August, less than four weeks before the killings. In this instance his custodial sentence was to be followed by one year's community supervision. As a consequence Zamora had been checking in to the Department of Corrections regularly and had passed drug and alcohol tests as recently as 21 August.

However, Zamora was now charged with 20 felony counts which included six counts of aggravated first-degree murder that could bring the death sentence. At his first hearing, Zamora mumbled 'Guilty, guilty, guilty, guilty' as he entered.

'Can you hear me? I'm guilty,' he told Skagit County Superior Court. However, the public defender Keith Tyne said that it was clear that Zamora had significant mental

VICTIMS

Julie Binschus, 48
Greg Gillum, 38
Sheriff's Deputy Anne Jackson, 40
Leroy Lange, 64
David Radcliffe, 58
Chester Rose, 58

CONNIE HICKMAN

Around 2000 Zamora met Connie Hickman when they were both working at a health-care facility. They began going out, but he had trouble holding down jobs. He would make threats and start fights over things that never happened, Hickman said. Initially, she attributed this to Zamora's drinking and drug use.

After several suicide attempts, Zamora told Hickman that he was hearing voices. In 2003 Hickman and Dennise Zamora took him to Whatcom County hospital, saying they feared for their safety. He was diagnosed with both bipolar disorder and schizophrenia, and was held there for several weeks before being discharged. 'The night after he was released, he called me and said, "I want to go back,"' Hickman said. But when he returned to the hospital, they refused to admit him.

Eventually, Zamora was admitted to another hospital. During that stay, court records showed he bit an orderly who was trying to restrain him.

After being released, Zamora stopped taking his medication. He did not have a job and could not afford to pay for it. His behaviour became increasingly volatile. Hickman dropped him, changed her phone number and took out a protection order. But he was able to track her down through friends. One night, after she bumped into him on the street, a wine bottle came flying through her apartment window. On another occasion, the windscreen of her roommate's car was smashed.

Hickman fled the state, but he tracked her down, leaving rambling messages on relatives' answering machines. However, she managed to elude him. Meanwhile, his family tried to get him back into treatment. But his trouble with the law continued.

health issues and he would defend him on that basis. Zamora's mother Dennise did not want to hear any excuses made for her son. 'I'm not one of those people who say he's not guilty by reason of insanity,' she said. 'He is guilty by reason of insanity.'

Friends said that, on good days, Zamora could be charming, warm and creative. But he could be strange, too. He would walk aimlessly around the streets alone at all hours or cause trouble by grabbing a fistful of paper towels from the petrol station and letting them trail out of the window of his car as he drove off. More recently though, they said, he had become increasingly scary.

Devious and vengeful

For ten years Zamora had shown signs of serious mental illness. Meanwhile, he racked up dozens of criminal charges. While none of them were for particularly violent offences, the state Department of Corrections had put him on a programme for offenders with mental illness. However, Zamora would not continue his mental-health treatment, despite his family's urgings, and the law prevented them from forcing him to do so.

In May 2007 he flew into a rage when a friend refused to go hiking with him and hurled a concrete block at the friend's car, damaging it. Zamora was charged with second-degree malicious mischief. In a statement to Skagit County Court, the friend described Zamora as 'devious and vengeful'. On 15 May he pleaded guilty. As part of his sentencing, he agreed not to possess firearms, although neighbours said he had a collection of six or seven guns.

MAMA'S BOY

There was little in Isaac Zamora's early life that indicated that he would become a spree killer. Friends who grew up with him remembered a sweet, sensitive mama's boy. His mother cosseted him. She taught him at home rather than sending him to school, while his father took him to Boy Scouts. Neighbour Christie Howard remembered him as a quiet, unremarkable kid. At worst, she recalled, he 'was one of the kids who rode his obnoxious motorcycle through the property'.

Then, when Zamora was about 14, the family home burned down and they lost everything. They struggled to cope both emotionally and financially. 'It's all we can do to keep the electricity on,' his mother wrote in the family's bankruptcy petition. Zamora was deeply affected. A doctor diagnosed that he was suffering from post-traumatic stress disorder and said that his problems would subside after puberty. But they did not.

The family stayed in the neighbourhood, living in a large mobile home on the site of their house. Around the same time, Zamora stole his mother's gun to sell it to another teenager. He was later charged with filing a false report after telling police that a stranger had stolen it.

In 2001 Zamora and a friend were accused of stealing an outboard motor. Zamora refused to co-operate with the Mount Vernon Police Department who were investigating the theft. But his mother got into his room by climbing through the window of the trailer, found the outboard motor and turned it over to police. Zamora pleaded guilty to second-degree theft and served three days in jail plus 17 days community service.

It transpired that the guns he used in his killing spree were stolen from a house near his mother's home. After Zamora was released from jail, his parents threw him out and he began sleeping outdoors in the woods and then on neighbours' lawns. The week just before his murder spree, he told neighbour Shirley Wenrick: 'I am going to get even with them.'

On his release, he had agreed to take the first of two evaluations he needed to qualify for state mental-health programmes. However, since he did not have the money to pay for this, the Department of Corrections had to go to the state's Department of Social and Health Services for the financing. All this bureaucracy took time and by the time the first of his evaluations was scheduled, it was too late for Zamora and his victims.

Not guilty by reason of insanity

Although he still had enough sense to hand himself in after the spree, by the time Zamora got to court his condition had deteriorated further. At a hearing on 5 September, he said: 'I kill for God. I listen to God.' Through a plea bargain at his trial he was found not guilty by reason of insanity of two of the murders while pleading guilty to the other four. This meant that he could be held in a mental institution rather than face execution, but that, because of his guilty plea in connection with the other four murders, he could be transferred to a prison if his mental health issues were resolved. Zamora was confined at Western State Hospital and placed under 24-hour guard by two Department of Corrections SWAT team members.

MATTI JUHANI SAARI

Just ten months after the massacre at Jokela High School, the police were investigating whether there had been any communication between Pekka-Eric Auvinen and Matti Juhani Saari, the 22-year-old catering student who killed ten in the Kauhajoki High School shooting in western Finland.

At about 10.40 a.m. on 23 September 2008 a man wearing a ski-mask appeared in a classroom in the middle of an exam and started shooting. Then he threw a petrol bomb, setting the classroom on fire. Apparently, Saari had entered the school buildings via the basement and concealed himself until roughly 200 people were inside the building. Armed with a .22-calibre Walther P22 semi-automatic pistol, he walked calmly through the classroom, approaching his victims individually before shooting them. He seemed to be revelling in his actions. Some students escaped by jumping from windows. They were hindered by a river that ran behind the school and took to rowing boats to make their getaway.

After around five minutes Saari ran down a corridor and threw a petrol bomb into a language laboratory. He then shot out all of the windows in the school's main corridor and took aim at the janitor Jukka Forsberg, who escaped by ducking and weaving to avoid the shots.

'I saw a guy leaving a big black bag in the corridor and going into classroom number three and closing the door,' Forsberg said. 'I looked through the window and he immediately shot at me. Then I called the emergency number. Thank God I was not hit, he fired at me but I was running zigzag. I ran for my life.' Forsberg heard constant shooting. 'He changed another case in the gun. He was very well prepared. He walked calmly.'

At around 11 a.m. the police arrived. As they entered the yard of the college Saari shot at them and they were forced to retreat. Forty-five minutes later more police units turned up in armoured vehicles. They attempted to enter the building through the main corridor, but were forced back by black smoke.

When they finally gained entry at around 12.30 p.m., they found Saari in the main corridor with a gunshot wound to the head. They rushed him to Tampere University Hospital, where he died at 4.46 that afternoon.

A record death toll

Nine bodies were found in the exam room, some so badly burned that they could only be identified from DNA and dental records. Another was found in the nearby corridor, shot down after fleeing the burning classroom. Most victims suffered multiple gunshot wounds; one as many as 20. Eight of the victims were female students. One was a male student.

All were in their twenties and were classmates of Saari's. The tenth was a teacher in his fifties. Another 21-year-old woman was shot in the head but recovered after two operations. A further ten students were treated for minor injuries including sprains

NORTHERN ILLINOIS UNIVERSITY SHOOTING

Sadly, spree killings in schools and universities are a regular event in the USA. On 14 February 2008 27-year-old Steven Kazmierczak, a former student, entered a lecture hall at Northern Illinois University in DeKalb and opened fire on a crowd of students with a shotgun and three handguns. He killed six and wounded 18, then took his own life when the police turned up. Kazmierczak was said to have been an 'outstanding student'. His girlfriend said that he had never shown any violent tendencies previously, though three weeks before the shooting he had stopped taking Prozac, which had been prescribed to him by a psychiatrist.

The Northern Illinois University shooting was the fourth-deadliest university shooting in US history, after Virginia Tech, the Austin clock-tower shootings and the California State University library massacre in 1976, when paranoid schizophrenic Edward Allaway claimed staff members were watching pornographic movies. He believed that pornographers were forcing his estranged wife to appear in their films. Allaway was confined in Patton State Hospital in San Bernardino.

and cuts from broken glass. With ten dead, Saari had clocked up the highest death toll of any peacetime attack in Finnish history. But it could have been so much worse. Saari had fired a total of nearly 200 shots, some aimed harmlessly in the air.

The male student who died was thought to have been a close friend of Saari's. The pair had spent an evening out together in February 2008 when they were threatened with a starting pistol. A photo of them together had been circulating on the Internet, where Saari was jokingly pointing at his friend's head with his forefinger.

Two days after the killings, a friend of Saari's, named Rauno, told a magazine that he had received a call from Saari at 11.53 a.m. on the day of the massacre when Saari confessed to having killed ten people. He quite calmly told Rauno that he was calling to say goodbye.

Saari left behind two handwritten notes in his school dormitory, saying that he had been planning the massacre for six years. His motive for the shooting was, he said: 'I hate the human race ... The solution is Walther 22.' But that was not how people remembered him. Former classmate Susanna Keronen said: 'He was happy, a social guy – there was nothing exceptional – and he got along with people well and he was not lonely. He had friends.'

YouTube

In the weeks leading up to the massacre, Saari had posted several videos on YouTube showing him firing a handgun at a local shooting range. These were accompanied by the quote: 'Whole life is war and whole life is pain. And you will fight alone in your personal war.' These are lyrics from the song 'War' by the Bavarian band :wumpscut:. Among his video favourites he included footage of the Columbine High School

SANNA SILLANPÄÄ

In 1999 30-year-old Finnish woman Sanna Riitta Liisa Sillanpää a computer science graduate, rented a pistol at a shooting club in Helsinki and shot three men dead and wounded another. Among the dead were the club's 23-year-old supervisor. As Sillanpää was leaving the club, she said: 'This is what they taught us at the FBI academy, isn't it?'

She then travelled to the Helsinki-Vantaa Airport in a bus, carrying the gun with her. After buying a ticket to London, she dropped the gun in a rubbish bin where it was found by a cleaner. She was arrested soon afterwards as she boarded the plane.

In court Sillanpää refused to speak and no motive for the shooting was discovered. She was later found to be suffering from paranoid schizophrenia.

Under Finnish law she was judged to be partially insane and tried. She was found guilty on three counts of manslaughter and two counts of attempted manslaughter, and incarcerated in the mental hospital in Kuopio in Finland.

massacre and he listed his interests as 'horror movies, guns, sex, beer and computers'. The police had received an anonymous tip-off about his website on the Friday before the shooting. They talked to Saari and searched his home on the day before the incident, but found no reason to arrest him as he had a temporary weapons permit. But the police did not know about another video Saari had posted on a Finnish social networking site, where he pointed a gun at the camera and said, in English: 'You will die next.' Then he fired four shots in the direction of the camera. The police said that they would have detained Saari if they had known about this second video when they had questioned him. They also believed Saari's videos were shot by someone else, most probably the male friend Saari murdered in the massacre.

The police noted the similarities between the Auvinen and Saari massacres. They had bought their guns from the same store. Both had taken photographs of themselves in similar poses. They both had been part of an Internet group, which used YouTube and Finnish social networking site IRC-Galleria. Users of this site, which included people from Finland, Germany and the USA, exchanged videos related to school shootings. Jari Neulaniemi, the detective leading the Kauhajoki investigation, said that it was 'very likely' that the two men had been in contact at some point.

Mixed motives

Although most of Saari's victims were female, the motive did not seem to be a hatred of women. Rauno said Saari had opted for a catering course so that he would be surrounded by female students. However, Saari had also told Rauno that he had been the victim of bullying in secondary school. Saari's behaviour had begun to worry Rauno over two years before the shootings. He had begun expressing a fondness for guns and an interest in the school shootings in the USA. Around 18 months before the massacre, Saari had sent Rauno a message saying that he was going to carry out a school shooting the next day, though in fact he only bought the handgun in August 2008, a month before the massacre.

TIM KRETSCHMER

Germany, 11 March 2009

Roll-call of death

On the morning of 11 March 2009 17-year-old Tim Kretschmer took a 9mm Beretta semi-automatic pistol from his parents' bedroom and returned to the Albertville technical school in Winnenden, Baden-Württemberg, Germany, which he had left the previous year. Arriving there at approximately 9.30 a.m., he made for the classrooms and chemistry laboratory on the first floor. There he killed one female teacher and nine students – one male and eight female – shooting them in the head. As most of his victims were female, it seemed that he was specifically targeting women and girls.

Kretschmer was dressed in a black combat uniform, but he was immediately recognized by teachers and former classmates. After the Erfurt school massacre in April 2002, a coded message had been devised to warn staff of danger. The headmaster broadcast over the school Tannoy: 'Mrs Koma is coming' – 'Koma' being 'amok' in reverse. Hearing the announcement, the teachers locked their classroom doors.

In response to an emergency call, three police officers reached the scene at 9.35 a.m. They entered the school and interrupted Kretschmer's shooting spree. He shot at them and fled, killing two more female teachers in the hallway. Kretschmer escaped through the garden of a nearby psychiatric hospital, where he had earlier been treated, killing the hospital's 56-year-old janitor on the way.

VICTIMS

Jacqueline Hahn, 16
Ibrahim Halilaj, 17
Franz Josef Just, 56
Stefanie Tanja Kleisch, 16
Michaela Köhler, 26
Selina Marx, 15
Nina Denise Mayer, 24
Viktorija Minasenko, 16
Nicole Elisabeth Nalepa, 17
Denis Puljic, 36
Chantal Schill, 15
Jana Natascha Schober, 15
Sabrina Schüle, 24
Kristina Strobel, 16
Sigurt Peter Gustav Wilk, 46

'Mrs Koma' hijacks a car

At around 10 a.m. Kretschmer carjacked a Volkswagen minivan at a car park in Winnenden. Sitting in the rear seat, he ordered the driver, Igor Wolf, at gunpoint to take him to Wendlingen, an hour from Winnenden. During the trip, Kretschmer revealed his chilling intentions. While reloading his pistol magazines, he said: 'Do you think we will still find another school?' Wolf quickly changed the conversation and took a circuitous route, hoping to stall him. Just after midday they approached the turn-off to Wendlingen. Spotting a police patrol car, Wolf seized the opportunity to steer the van on to the grass verge and jumped from the vehicle. Kretschmer quickly abandoned the van too and ran towards the nearby industrial area.

He entered a Volkswagen car showroom and demanded the keys for one of the cars. The salesman managed to escape while the gunman was distracted. Kretschmer then shot and killed one of the other salesmen and a customer, firing 13 bullets into the two people. As he reloaded, another salesman and visitor fled through the rear exit.

Kretschmer emerged from the showroom at about 12.30 p.m. and shot at a passing car, but the driver escaped without injury. Then the police arrived and a shootout started. Injured, the gunman took cover back in the car showroom, firing 12 shots at the police. While the police were trying to surround the building, Kretschmer escaped out of the back. He ran across a yard to a neighbouring business complex where he shot and injured two police officers in an unmarked police car.

Kretschmer continued to shoot at random at nearby buildings and people. He then reloaded his pistol and shot himself in the head. During the whole shooting spree the gunman fired a total of 112 rounds – 60 in the school which was his primary target.

EMSDETTEN SCHOOL SHOOTING

At 9.30 a.m. on 20 November 2006 18-year-old former student Sebastian Bosse entered Geschwister School in Emsdetten, northwest Germany, fired several shots and set off smoke grenades. Eight people were injured including three students, a teacher and a janitor. Bosse was later found dead with a self-inflicted gunshot wound to the head. He had been carrying two sawn-off shotguns and had a knife strapped to his leg. Homemade pipe bombs were lying nearby and he had other explosive devices on his body.

Bosse had posted a suicide note on the Internet, saying that he hated people and had been taught to be a 'loser' at his school. It was also discovered that Bosse spent most of his waking hours playing a violent video game, *Counter-Strike*. There have been calls for such games to be banned.

Beretta at large

Police had raided the Kretschmer family house at about 11 a.m. on the day of the shooting. Kretschmer's father was a member of a local marksmen's club and owned, legally, 15 guns. Fourteen of these firearms were kept in a gun safe, while the Beretta his son had taken was kept unsecured in the bedroom. Several hundred rounds of ammunition were also found to be missing.

In November 2009 the Public Prosecutor's Department in Stuttgart indicted Kretschmer's father on charges of negligent homicide, bodily injury caused by negligence and violation of the weapons laws. His guns were confiscated, though Kretschmer senior had already announced that he would voluntarily relinquish his gun ownership. Kretschmer had taken his son to the gun club to 'share the thrill of high-calibre weapons,' neighbours said.

Tim Kretschmer was described as a 'lonely and frustrated person' by a friend. He had graduated from Albertville technical school in 2008 with poor grades that

THE ERFURT MASSACRE

On 26 April 2002 19-year-old Robert Steinhäuser armed himself with a 9mm Glock 17 semi-automatic pistol and a 12-gauge pump-action shotgun and returned to Johann Gutenberg school in Erfurt, which had just expelled him. He went into the toilet to change into a black combat outfit – like the one that Kretschmer would later wear – and a 'ninja-style' mask. Around 11.05 a.m. he came out shooting.

Steinhäuser moved from classroom to classroom shooting the teachers. However, two students were also killed when he fired through a locked door. The police turned up at about 11.10 a.m., and Steinhäuser shot an officer in the head, killing him. Steinhäuser was then confronted by Rainer Heise, one of his teachers, who grabbed him by the shirt and tried to talk to him. 'He then pulled off his mask and I said, "Robert?",' Heise said. 'I said go ahead and shoot me, but look me in the face.'

Steinhäuser replied: 'That's it for today.' Heise then pushed him into a room and locked the door. Shortly afterwards Steinhäuser shot himself. By then he had killed 16 people. During his 20-minute frenzy he had fired 40 rounds from the Glock pistol but had not used the shotgun. A marksman at a local gun club, he was carrying both guns legally. He owned two others. He was also carrying around 1,000 rounds of ammunition, which was enough to kill hundreds of people.

prevented him taking up an apprenticeship. He had ambitions to become a professional table tennis player, though his high opinion of his own abilities caused him to denigrate those of his team mates. When his coach took this up with his mother, she sided with her son. He was a 'mummy's boy', the coach concluded.

Kretschmer staged shootouts with air pistols in a nearby forest. He was a devotee of video games and played a first-person shooter game the day before he died. His computer revealed that he also enjoyed watching sadomasochistic movies where a man is tied up and humiliated by women. He had watched one the evening before the shooting.

In 2008 Kretschmer had been treated for clinical depression as an in-patient at Weissenhof Psychiatric Clinic in nearby Heilbronn, then as an out-patient in Winnenden, though he stopped the treatment. Three weeks before the shooting, a friend said that Kretschmer had written to his parents saying that he was suffering and could not go on. An Internet blog purporting to have been posted by Kretschmer and explaining why he had carried out the shooting proved to be a forgery.

Violent games

The families of five victims wrote an open letter to Chancellor Angela Merkel and other politicians, calling for the government to stop youths going to gun clubs, for less violence on television and for the banning of violent video games. In June 2009 the German government passed legislation to increase the age limit for large-calibre weapons and start a nationwide electronic weapons registry to improve handgun security, as well as instituting random inspections of gun owners' homes.

JIVERLY ANTARES WONG

USA, 3 April 2009

'America sucks'

Forty-one-year-old Jiverly Antares Wong was a naturalized US citizen with a grudge. Some time before 10.30 a.m. on 3 April 2009 he blocked the rear door of the American Civic Association immigration centre in Binghamton, upstate New York, with a vehicle registered in his father's name. Wearing a bulletproof vest covered by a bright green nylon jacket, Wong entered the building through the front door, shooting at anyone who got in his way.

His first victim was one of the Civic Association's receptionists. Without saying a word, he went up to the reception desk and shot her in the head. He then shot the other receptionist, Shirley DeLucia, in the stomach. She feigned death. When the gunman moved on, she took cover under a desk and called the emergency services on 911. The call was logged at 10.38 a.m. She then stayed on the line for 39 minutes and relayed information until she was rescued.

Welcome to America!

Wong walked into an English-language lesson in the citizenship class, just off the main reception area, and continued shooting. Everyone in the classroom suffered a gunshot wound. When Wong heard the police sirens, he turned his gun on himself. In a matter of minutes he had fired 99 rounds; 88 from a 9mm Beretta and 11 from a .45-calibre Beretta, killing 13 people. It was likely that he knew some of the fellow immigrants he shot in the citizenship class.

Among the wounded was 42-year-old Vietnamese immigrant Long Huynh, who had tried to shield his wife Lan Ho. A bullet that first shattered Huynh's elbow ricocheted, striking his wife and killing her.

When the police arrived they did not know whether the gunman was alive or dead. They locked down nearby Binghamton High School and a number of surrounding streets. Learning that the perpetrator was Vietnamese, they called in Broome Community College assistant professor Tuong Hung Nguyen, who was fluent in the language.

A SWAT team was sent in and began clearing the building at 11.13 a.m. They proceeded with caution as Wong's suicide had not been confirmed. A number of people had taken refuge in the basement and in a closet, and it was feared that the gunman had taken hostages. It was not until after midday that Wong was found dead in an office on the first floor of the building.

He was found to have two semi-automatic Berettas that matched the serial numbers on his New York State pistol licence. A hunting knife was found tucked in his waistband and a bag of ammunition was

> **'Already impartial now … cop bring about this shooting … cop must responsible. And you have a nice day.'**

tied around his neck. A number of unspent magazines were also found at the scene along with a laser sight. A few days after the incident an envelope was delivered to News 10 Now, a TV station in Syracuse, upstate New York. The letter was dated 18 March 2009 but the envelope was postmarked 3 April 2009, the day of the shootings. The envelope contained a two-page handwritten letter, photos of Wong smiling and holding his guns, a gun permit and Wong's driver's licence.

On the rampage

Wong's sister said that she had no idea that her brother was going to go on the rampage. They did not live together, but she spoke to him on the phone at least once a week. Wong had come to North America in the 1980s, living in New York, California and, briefly, Canada. He was naturalized in the USA in 1995.

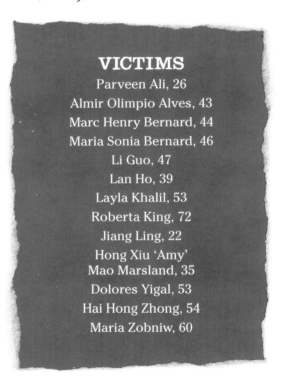

VICTIMS
Parveen Ali, 26
Almir Olimpio Alves, 43
Marc Henry Bernard, 44
Maria Sonia Bernard, 46
Li Guo, 47
Lan Ho, 39
Layla Khalil, 53
Roberta King, 72
Jiang Ling, 22
Hong Xiu 'Amy'
Mao Marsland, 35
Dolores Yigal, 53
Hai Hong Zhong, 54
Maria Zobniw, 60

In Los Angeles he worked for seven years as a delivery man for the catering company Kikka Sushi. During his time there he married and divorced, but the couple had no children. He also picked up a misdemeanour conviction for fraud. After he moved to Binghamton in upstate New York, Wong worked at a local Shop-Vac vacuum cleaner plant until it closed in November 2008.

To Wong's former co-workers and those who knew him, his killing spree was less of a surprise. 'From the people close to him, this action he took was not a surprise to them,' said local Binghamton Police Chief Joseph Zikuski. 'Apparently people were making fun of him. He felt degraded from his inability to speak English and he was upset about that.'

Wong had also allegedly made comments such as 'America sucks' and talked about assassinating the president to his former co-workers at Shop Vac. He had recently lost his job and was having difficulties finding another one.

However, one of his former co-workers told CNN: 'He was quiet – not a violent person ... I can't believe he would do something like this.'

In addition to the 14 people Wong killed, he also wounded several other people. Among them were Shirley DeLucia, aged 61, the Civic Association receptionist who feigned death and then managed to contact the police even though she was critically wounded.

Wong's twisted hatred of the country that had given him a new life ensured that the American dream was brought to a tragic and sudden end for many in the Civic

THE LETTER

Wong wrote to the TV station News 10 Now in an attempt to explain his actions. The letter was hand-written, largely in capital letters. He apologized for his poor English. The letter read:

'Date: March – 18 – 2009

Dear: New 10 Now

I am Jiverly Wong shooting the people

The first I want to say sorry I know a little English I hope you understand all of this. Of course you need to know why I shooting? Because undercover cop gave me a lot of ass during eighteen years. I got seven years and eight month delivery to grocery in the California. Came back New York on the August – 2007. Let talk about when I live in California such as … cop used 24 hours the technique of ultramodern and camera for burn the chemical in my house. For switch the channel TiVi. For adjust the fan. For made me unbreathble. For made me vomit. For connect the music into my ear.

Undercover cop usual coined some nasty was not true about me and spread a rumor to the receiver and some people know me conduce toward many people prejudiced and selfish to me … cop made me lost my job … cop put me became poor.

Let talk about when I live at the 28. Baker. St. 2nd floor. Johnson City. New York 13790. It terrible when I live there such as … cop wait until midnight when I off the light and went to the bed. Cop unlock my door and came in take a sit in my room << cop did it thirteen time on the year 1994 >> on the thirteen time had three time touch me when I sleeping. One time stolen 20 dollar in my wallet one time used electric gun shoot at the behind my neck. (That time I did not know English)

Please continue second page thank you.

[Page 2]

From 1990 to 1995 New York undercover cop try to get a car accident with me. Such as when I driving on the highway and on the street undercover cop sundennly brake the car stop immediately at the of front my car … cop did it 32 time like that during 1990 to 1995 but I never hit the car.

Many time from 1990 to 1997 at the day time … cop exploit unknon English and went to my house knock the door for harass and domineer. Of course during that time cop coined something was not true about me and spread a rumor nasty like the California cop.

From August – 2007 until now cop gave me not to much ass only one time cop leave a massage in my voice mail and said << come back your country >> after five minute I send a text massage to them I said I will call the police and they send it back to me they said they are the police.

Dear. New Ten Now. Right now I still get unemploment benefit of the company Shop Vac Endicott. New York State Department of Labor was cheat and unpaid from December – 1st – 2008 to December – 28th – 2008. I already claim weekly benefit from that date. Any way I can not accepted my poor life. Before I cut my poor life I must oneself get a judge job for make an impartial with undercover cop by at least two people with me go to return to the dust of earth.'

Association that day. As for Long Huynh, the Vietnamese immigrant whose wife had been killed, in addition to the injury to his elbow, one of his fingers was shot off and a bullet hit his chest. Another bullet entered his chin and exited through his cheek. With his wife dead, he later said he wished he had died too and only continued to live for the sake of their two children.

NIDAL MALIK HASAN

USA, 5 November 2009

The Fort Hood shootings

A shooting that touched a nerve across America was the massacre at Fort Hood during which US Army psychiatrist Nidal Malik Hasan shot a number of soldiers who were about to be deployed in Iraq and Afghanistan. A Muslim of Palestinian descent, Hasan had expressed radical beliefs and had connections to Anwar al-Awlaki, a recruiter for al-Qaeda who had preached to at least three of the 9/11 terrorists.

Hasan worked at the Soldier Readiness Center at Fort Hood, where military personnel received routine medical checks before a deployment and immediately on their return. On 5 November 2009 he arrived at work around 1.20 p.m. and took a seat at an empty table. Hasan bowed his head for several seconds and then jumped onto a desk and shouted: 'Allahu Akbar!' – 'God is great' – before producing two pistols. One of them was a FN Herstal 'Five-seveN' semi-automatic pistol, which one firearms website describes as capable of defeating 'most body armour in military service around the world today'. He had bought it in a civilian store. The other was a .357 Magnum revolver which he held in reserve.

The shots came so rapidly that Private Marquest Smith, who was going over some paperwork in a cubicle in the building, thought at first the sound was microwave popcorn. Then someone shouted: 'Gun!'

Shooting methodically

Private Smith dived under a desk. He stayed there for several minutes, before making a dash for safety. As he broke for the door, he saw Hasan in combat fatigues, moving around the room. His handgun was pointed downwards and he was methodically shooting the soldiers who were already on the ground or were crouching down, seeking cover. As Private Smith fled, a bullet hit his boot. It stuck in the sole of the boot, but he was uninjured.

Hasan moved on to fire at a crowd that had gathered for a college graduation ceremony scheduled in a nearby theatre. He appeared to concentrate on soldiers in uniform and fired more than 100 rounds. 'He looked extremely focused,' said Francisco De La Serna, a 23-year-old medic who fled the building. Although they were on an army base, none of the soldiers were armed. However, Kimberly Munley, a 35-year-old

VICTIMS
Michael Grant Cahill, 62
L. Eduardo Caraveo, 52
Justin Michael DeCrow, 32
John P. Gaffaney, 56
Frederick Greene, 29
Jason Dean Hunt, 22
Amy Sue Krueger, 29
Aaron Thomas Nemelka, 19
Michael S. Pearson, 22
Russell Gilbert Seager, 51
Francheska Velez, 21
Juanita L. Warman, 55
Kham See Xiong, 23

ANWAR AL-AWLAKI

Radical preacher Anwar al-Awlaki has been described as the 'bin Laden of the Internet'. Nidal Malik Hasan attended his sermons, along with three of the 9/11 hijackers. Al-Awlaki left the USA in 2004 and moved to London, where it is thought he had contact with Umar Farouk Abdulmutallab, the suspect in the Northwest Airlines Flight terrorist attack over Detroit on Christmas Day 2009. In 2004 he moved to Yemen. He was arrested in 2006 but released after 18 months. By December 2009 he was back on the Yemeni government's most-wanted list.

Between December 2008 and June 2009, US intelligence intercepted 18 emails between Hasan and al-Awlaki. In one Hasan wrote: 'I can't wait to join you [in the afterlife].' After the Fort Hood shooting, al-Awlaki praised Hasan as a hero. He said: 'Nidal opened fire on soldiers who were on their way to be deployed to Iraq and Afghanistan. How can there be any dispute about the virtue of what he has done? In fact the only way a Muslim could Islamically justify serving as a soldier in the US army is if his intention is to follow the footsteps of men like Nidal.'

police officer, happened to be nearby. She was waiting for her squad car to get a tune-up when she heard the commotion and raced to the scene.

As she rounded a corner, she saw Hasan chasing a wounded soldier through an open courtyard as though he was trying to finish him off. Sergeant Munley's first shot missed Hasan. He spun round to face her. The two of them then had a running gun battle. Munley took two bullets to her legs. Both entered her left thigh, ripped through the flesh and lodged in her right thigh. She also received a minor wound to the right wrist.

'Just turned and fired'

By then a 911 call had been made and Sergeant Mark Todd, another civilian police officer, arrived and fired at Hasan. 'He was firing at people as they were trying to run and hide,' said Todd. 'Then he turned and fired a couple of rounds at me. I didn't hear him say a word, he just turned and fired.' Hasan was felled by shots from Todd, who then kicked a pistol out of his hand and placed him in handcuffs.

Specialist De La Serna, who had taken cover across the street, sprinted to the scene as the shooting stopped and put a tourniquet on Munley, who faded in and out of consciousness. Then he moved to Hasan, who had a gunshot wound through the chest. Hasan was calm and quiet, conscious but very weak. He had a handgun at his side and the pockets of his combat fatigues were full of extra magazines for his pistol.

As soon as the shooting stopped, soldiers in the processing centre shifted into combat mode, ripping up their uniforms to use as tourniquets. The wounded flooded into the emergency room on the base, where nurses and doctors struggled to cope with the volume of injuries. Munley was rushed to hospital and underwent surgery to halt the bleeding.

The incident had lasted about ten minutes. It resulted in 30 people being wounded and 13 killed – 12 soldiers and one civilian. Eleven died at the scene; two died later in

THE MAKING OF A KILLER

Nidal Malik 'AbduWali' Hasan was born in 1970 in Arlington, Virginia, to Palestinian parents who had emigrated from the West Bank. He joined the US Army from high school. He served eight years as an enlisted soldier while attending college. After graduating from Virginia Tech in 1995 with a bachelor's degree in biochemistry, he went to medical school, and qualified as an MD in 2003. He then completed a residency in psychiatry at Walter Reed Army Medical Center.

In June 2007, at the culmination of his residency, he was supposed to make a presentation on a medical topic of his choosing. Instead he gave a talk called 'The Koranic World View as it Relates to Muslims in the US Military'.

'It's getting harder and harder for Muslims in the service to morally justify being in a military that seems constantly engaged against fellow Muslims,' he said, and he suggested that to avoid 'adverse events' the military should allow Muslim soldiers to be released as conscientious objectors instead of fighting in wars against other Muslims. He made several references to Osama bin Laden, the Taliban, suicide bombers and Iran. The talk was not well received.

His cousin said that Hasan was harassed by his fellow soldiers because of his religion. In August 2009 his car was vandalized – neighbours said it was because he was a Muslim. It was part of Hasan's job to offer counselling to those who had returned from Iraq and Afghanistan. The stories he heard turned him against the wars. Hasan himself was due to be sent to Afghanistan on 28 November 2009.

hospital. The dead included one teenager, 19-year-old Aaron Nemelka, who had joined the army the previous year straight out of high school. Twenty-two-year-old Specialist Jason Dean Hunt had just married and Francheska Velez, a 21-year-old oil-tank driver who had completed tours in Korea and Iraq, was two months pregnant with her first child when she died. Five army reservists were also killed, including Michael Cahill, who was 62 and worked at the processing centre as a physician's assistant.

Hasan was taken to Brooke Army Medical Center in Fort Sam Houston, Texas, where he was held under heavy guard. He had been hit by at least four shots and was paralysed. He refused to talk to investigators.

Death penalty

Hassan was charged with 13 counts of premeditated murder and 32 counts of attempted murder within the military's legal system, making him eligible for the death penalty if convicted. In April 2010, he was moved to the Bell County Jail in Belton, Texas. Fort Hood negotiated a renewable $207,000 contract with Bell County in March to house Hasan for six months. The army also imposed restrictions on Hasan that he speak

'We love death more than you love life'

only in English on the phone or with visitors unless an interpreter is present. The army prosecutor has given formal notice that he will be seeking the death penalty in this case.

IBRAHIM SHKUPOLLI

Finland, 31 December 2009

The Sello mall shooting

Not surprisingly, the locations favoured by spree killers are those where groups of people congregate. So postmen and other office workers go on the rampage in their workplace and students shoot their fellows in schools and universities. The other places that crazed gunmen most often choose for their massacres are shopping malls.

On 31 December 2009 43-year-old Ibrahim Shkupolli discovered that his ex-girlfriend had a lover in the grocery store where she worked, in the Sello Prisma hypermarket in the Leppävaara district of Espoo, Finland's second largest city, located a short drive west of Helsinki. He went to her apartment and brutally stabbed her to death. Then he headed to the mall, where there were between 2,000 and 3,000 people shopping.

Dressed all in black, Shkupolli arrived at the Prisma hypermarket at 10.08 a.m. He went up to the second floor and opened fire with a 9mm handgun. Then he moved down to the first floor, continuing his killing spree. He killed three men and one woman, all employees of Prisma. It was believed that his ex-girlfriend's lover was among the victims. The female victim was shot twice in the stomach, the men in the head. The victims were aged between 27 and 45. 'There were loads of people who were crying, and many salespeople who were completely panicked,' a witness said.

Covered in blood

A woman told a news reporter that she had seen the suspect carrying a long-barrelled pistol, rushing past the cashier line at the hypermarket, where the murders took place. Another witness said he saw one worker lying on the floor covered in blood. Hundreds of shop workers were evacuated to a nearby library and fire station, and the mall was cordoned off. Shkupolli had disappeared and the police began a major manhunt. Trains were halted at nearby Leppävaara railway station and helicopters were brought in as police scoured the area.

Several hours later, Shkupolli was found dead in an apartment in Kirstinmäki, Espoo, where he had apparently committed suicide. Later the police went to his ex-girlfriend's flat and found her body. She was 32.

Ibrahim Shkupolli had been born in Mitrovica, Kosovo, in 1966. He moved to Finland in 1990. For 28 years he maintained a relationship with a Finnish girl, both before and after his marriage to an Albanian woman who bore him three children. Shkupolli had a job in a warehousing company, organizing deliveries to the Prisma shop. His employer did not notice anything out of the ordinary in his behaviour prior to the shootings.

However, his girlfriend had filed charges about his behaviour. She claimed that he had threatened to kill her. The courts had imposed a restraining order, banning Shkupolli from approaching her or her workplace. He had been convicted of assault, possession of a handgun and ammunition, as well as possession of narcotics. He was also under investigation for human trafficking from the Balkans to Finland and his application for Finnish citizenship had been rejected. The head of the Asylum Unit of the Finnish Immigration Service, Esko Repo, said he should have been deported. The police believed that Shkupolli's rampage was sparked by his jealousy. 'The four victims in the shopping centre were, in a way, outsiders,' said Chief Inspector Jukka Kaski. 'It looks like the incident is linked to the fifth victim. She seems to have been the gunman's main target and the whole shooting is tied up with the relationship between her and the gunman.'

THE TROLLEY SQUARE SHOOTING

At 6.44 p.m. on 12 February 2007 18-year-old Sulejman Talovic, an immigrant from Bosnia Herzegovina, went to the Trolley Square Mall in Salt Lake City, Utah, his regular hangout. But that evening he was carrying a shotgun, a handgun and a backpack full of ammunition. He shot and killed five people and injured another four. Off-duty policeman Kenneth Hammond was in the mall with his pregnant wife Sarita, a 911 dispatcher. While Hammond traded shots with Talovic, his wife borrowed a mobile phone from a waiter and put in a 911 call. A SWAT team arrived and a marksman shot and killed Talovic.

There is some suggestion that Talovic suffered from a mental illness, having lived in Sarajevo during the Bosnian War. He is also alleged to have shouted 'Allahu Akbar!' ('God is the Greatest!') during the shooting. However, his father blamed the American government.

'In the US, you cannot buy cigarettes if you are under-aged, but you can buy a gun,' he said.

Stressed and armed

The Karolinska Institute in Stockholm conducted a large-scale survey of the mental health of Kosovo Albanians living in Sweden and found that many suffered from clinical depression and post-traumatic stress disorder. Similar findings have been made in other countries that took large numbers of Bosnian or Kosovan refugees during and after the Balkan wars. There seems to have been no follow-up study in Finland, which has been one of the strongest champions of an independent Kosovan statehood. Shkupolli does not appear to have ever been seen by a mental health professional.

After the Kauhajoki school shooting just 15 months before, the Finnish government had announced that all applicants to own a handgun had to provide a note from a doctor giving them a clean bill of mental health and be interviewed by the police. The gun Shkupolli used in his shooting spree was unlicensed.

With a population of 5.3 million, Finland has 1.6 million firearms in private hands. The country has deep-rooted hunting traditions and ranks among the top three nations in the world for civilian gun ownership. This incident was Finland's third major shooting in two years. Again politicians, social workers and religious leaders urged tighter gun laws and increased vigilance of Internet sites. There have also been calls for more social cohesion in the small Nordic nation, known for its high suicide rate, heavy drinking and domestic violence.

WESTROADS MALL SHOOTING

Nineteen-year-old Robert A. Hawkins had been plagued with mental problems throughout his short life. At the age of six he was hospitalized for depression. At 14 he was undergoing psychiatric treatment after threatening to kill his stepmother with an axe.

He then became a ward of the State of Nebraska and was hospitalized again with various disorders. He dropped out of school. Estranged from his parents, he went to live with two friends and their mother, Debora Maruca-Kovac, who described him as 'troubled'. He became depressed when he lost his job at McDonald's after being accused of stealing $17. Then he split up with his girlfriend.

Hawkins accused a local teenager of stealing his CD player and threatened to kill her. With one drug conviction already on his record, he had been arrested for delinquency and under-aged possession of alcohol on 24 November 2007. He was due to appear in court on 7 December. However, on 5 December, his mother found a suicide note. It read:

'Family

I'm so sorry for what I've put you through I never meant to hurt all of you so much and I don't blame any one of you for disowning me I just can't be a burden to you and my friends any longer You are all better off without me. I'm so sorry for this.

I've just snapped I can't take this meaningless existence anymore I've been a constant disappointment and that trend would have only continued. Just remember the good times we had together.

I love you mommy
I love you dad
I love you Kira
I love you Valancia
I love you Cynthia
I love you Zach
I love you Cayla
I love you Mark (P.S. I'm really sorry)

Friends

To all of my friends I'm so sorry for what I've done to you and put you through. I've been a peice of shit my entire life it seems this is my only option. I know everyone will remember me as some sort of monster but please understand that I just don't want to be a burden on the ones that I care for my entire life. I just want to take a few peices of shit with me. I love all of you so much and I don't want anyone to miss me just think about how much better you are off without me to support. I want my friends to remember all the good times we had together. Just think tho I'm gonna be fuckin famous. You guys have always been there for me I'm just sad that I'm gonna have to go this alone. You guys are the best friends anyone could ever ask for. That's all I have to say is that I fuckin love you guys.

P.S. I didn't eat that fuckin sandwich or the toilet thing either!

My will

I'm giving my car back to my mom and my friends can have whatever else I leave behind.'

He signed the note and attached his social security number.

An hour after his mother had delivered the note to the police, Hawkins walked into the Von Maur department store in the Westroads Mall in Omaha, Nebraska, with an AK-47 he had stolen from his stepfather's house. He killed eight people and wounded four others before turning the gun on himself.

CHRISTOPHER SPEIGHT

USA, 19 January 2010

The Appomattox County killings

Shortly after midday on 19 January 2010 an injured man was found beside a rural road in Appomattox County, Virginia. He was soaked in blood and lying face down. 'I knew something was really strange,' said 29-year-old Tammy Randolph, a neighbour of 39-year-old Christopher Speight and the woman who found the victim. She started running to Speight's house to call for help but turned back when she came across a second bloodied body in the road.

A deputy who went to investigate heard gunshots and retreated. When back-up officers arrived they found four dead bodies outside Speight's house. Another three bodies were found inside. The wounded man who had been found first was taken to hospital but was pronounced dead on arrival. There was no sign of Speight himself.

A manhunt began as over 100 police officers surrounded a wood to the west of Appomattox where the killer was thought to be hiding. A National Guard helicopter flying overhead was struck by gunfire and a bullet ruptured the fuel tank, forcing it to land. Dogs and thermal imaging units were brought in, and four local schools were closed. The police surrounded the wood, setting up a wide cordon around the perimeter, while gunfire was directed at them.

The following day at 7.10 a.m., after a 20-hour stand-off, Christopher Speight gave himself up to the police. He was wearing a bulletproof vest, but was not carrying the high-powered rifle which he was thought to have used to fire on the helicopter. He was charged with first-degree murder and taken to Blue Ridge Regional Jail in Lynchburg.

Speight was the co-owner of the house where the bodies were found. He had booby-trapped the property, but the explosives found inside and around the house were detonated safely by a bomb squad.

Chip on his shoulder

Co-workers said that Speight had seemed sullen and on edge during the days running up to the shooting. He worked as a security guard at a small grocery store. Speight was reported to have been distant since his mother had died of cancer in 2006, but he had more recently displayed increasing anger against family members who he believed were trying to steal the farmhouse that his mother had bequeathed to him and his sister. He feared the family were going to evict him.

VICTIMS
Lauralee Sipe, 38, Speight's sister
Morgan L. Dobyns, 15, Lauralee Sipe's daughter
Dwayne S. Sipe, 38, Lauralee Sipe's husband
Joshua Sipe, 4, the couple's son
Jonathan L. Quarles, 43
Karen Quarles, 43
Emily A. Quarles, 15
Ronald I. Scruggs II, 16

THE AMITYVILLE HORROR

The 1979 movie *The Amityville Horror* was inspired by events that took place five years before in Amityville, Long Island. On the evening of 13 November 1974 the Suffolk County Police Department received a call from a barman who said that a kid had just come into his bar saying that his entire family had been killed. When the police turned up at the address he gave in Ocean Avenue, Amityville, they found 23-year-old Ronald DeFeo Jr outside sobbing that his mother and father had been killed. Inside the police found the bodies not just of wealthy car dealer Ronald DeFeo Sr and his wife Louise, but also those of their other sons, seven-year-old John Matthew and 12-year-old Marc, and their daughters, Allison, 13, and Dawn, 18.

Ronald, it seemed, was the only survivor. He claimed that his family had been murdered by a friend of his father, Louis Falini, who DeFeo Jr had fallen out with over a botched paint job. Falini was a 'Mafia hitman' who had threatened to kill DeFeo's entire family. The police were unconvinced.

DeFeo Jr was a drug user with a criminal record and a history of violence. He was also a gun fanatic. A ballistics expert found that the victims had all been shot with a .35-calibre Marlin rifle. A box whose label showed that it had once contained a .35 Marlin was found in DeFeo Jr's bedroom. When challenged by the police DeFeo told several conflicting stories, but then he finally confessed.

'Once I started, I just could not stop,' he said.

Bad joke

'On Saturday, he was here,' said Tonya Maddox, a cashier at the store, 'and he wouldn't come inside. He wouldn't talk to anybody. We joked that he was going to shoot someone.'

Roger Harris, a 36-year-old mechanic and farmer who worked on the property next to Speight's, said he was accustomed to hearing guns. Speight was a gun enthusiast and enjoyed target shooting on a range on his property. But the shooting had become a daily occurrence shortly before the tragedy, with Speight firing high-powered rifles.

All of the dead were either family members or friends of the family. The last time Speight had been seen by many members of the family was at his mother's funeral.

'This is a horrific tragedy,' state police spokeswoman Corinne Geller said. 'It's definitely one of the worst mass killings in Virginia, probably since the Virginia Tech tragedy in April 2007.'

Speight had a learning disability and a history of mental problems and had run away from his sister Georgia's home during a breakdown in 2007. Lynchburg attorney Henry Devening, who handled legal matters for Speight's family, said he did not understand how Speight could have thought anyone was throwing him out. He added that Speight's sister had been trying to do right by him, signing a deed that put the Appomattox property in his name as their grandparents had requested in a 2006 trust.

'Lauralee was a great person,' he said. 'Very motivated to take care of the family. I can't imagine why he would turn on her.'

JAMES RUPPERT

Family rampages are not uncommon. On Easter Sunday 1975, the day after James Ruppert's 41st birthday, he was lying in bed nursing a hangover in the family home in Hamilton, Ohio. His widowed mother, 65-year-old Charity Ruppert, was downstairs preparing a big family meal. Her elder son Leonard, his wife Alma and their eight children – aged between four and 17 – were driving over from nearby Fairfield after morning mass.

At 4 p.m. James Ruppert came downstairs and chatted with his brother Leonard. The children were in the garden, hunting for Easter eggs. James said that he was going to do some target shooting and went upstairs to get his gun. When he came down again, he was carrying a rifle and three pistols. By this time the whole family was gathered in the kitchen.

'How's your Volkswagen?' Leonard asked his brother.

James answered with his gun. One shot sent Leonard tumbling from his seat. James then shot Alma. Charity Ruppert lunged at him in a desperate effort to save her grandchildren. She was the next to die. Then James killed the eight children one after the other.

Three hours later, James Ruppert picked up the phone and called the police. 'There's been a shooting here,' he said. When the police arrived they found six bloodstained bodies in the kitchen, five more in the lounge. There was no sign of a struggle. When he was arrested, Ruppert put up no resistance, but he refused to talk.

Ruppert was a sickly child, whose widowed mother lavished her love on her elder son Leonard. James claimed that his brother beat him and taunted him for his weediness. Leonard did better at school.

He went on to have a successful career with General Electric and a hugely successful family life, while James – now on the threshold of middle age – was a failure by comparison. Unable to hold down a job, he became a heavy drinker and was threatened with eviction by his mother.

James Ruppert began to believe that Leonard and his mother were involved in a conspiracy against him. They were whispering to the FBI that he was a communist and a homosexual. James's only comfort was his small collection of guns. He could be seen sitting on the river bank, taking pot-shots at floating tin cans with his .357 Magnum.

He also believed that his brother Leonard had been trying to sabotage his VW and his casual inquiry about the car sent Ruppert over the edge. He killed his brother along with his family so that they could never hurt him again.

At his trial Ruppert entered a plea of insanity. The prosecution challenged this. The motive for the murders, they said, was simple. Ruppert stood to inherit $300,000 in property, life assurance, investments and other savings. If found not guilty due to insanity, Ruppert would be sent to mental hospital. Sooner or later, he would be released to pick up the money. If he was found guilty of murder, the inheritance would be forfeit as he would not be allowed to benefit from his crime.

Ruppert was convicted on 11 counts of homicide and sentenced to life imprisonment. Later he was granted a new trial on a technicality. This time he was found guilty of the murders of his brother and mother, but not guilty on the nine other counts due to insanity. Even so, his inheritance was lost.

INDEX

**Main chapter names
are in bold**

INDEX